CHRIST ON CAMPUS

MEDITATIONS FOR COLLEGE LIFE

by DONALD L. DEFFNER

CONCORDIA PUBLISHING HOUSE · SAINT LOUIS

Concordia Publishing House, St. Louis, Mo.

Concordia Publishing House Ltd., London W. C. 1

© 1965 Concordia Publishing House

Library of Congress Catalog Card No. 65-24176

Manufactured in the United States of America

To Christina Corinne

Contents

Blues, Twentieth Century Blues, are getting me down.
Who's escaped those weary Twentieth Century blues?
Why, if there's a God in the sky, shouldn't He grin?
High above this dreary Twentieth Century din,
In this strange illusion, chaos and confusion,
People seem to lose their way.
What is there to strive for,
Love, or keep alive for — say?
Hey, hey, call it a day.
*Blues, nothing to win or lose.**

These words of Noel Coward aptly describe the temper of many collegians today. They live in a fast-moving world beset by a host of "leering images." There is the "identity crisis" to cope with: beyond discovering one's *self* in the heterogeneous Lonely Crowd, there is the choice of a career. Often it is a choice further complicated by pressure from parents who are using the student to achieve vicarious glory or to relive a college career they never finished or even had. For the girl there is the added specter of "senior clutch" — grasping at marriage just weeks away from graduation, when the diamonds begin to appear on dormmates' fingers at evening dinner.

And through it all, students seem to lose their way. Who am I? is the besetting question. And where is the church in all of this? Indeed, where is God Himself?

From Berkeley to Bronxville, from Ole Miss to Mizzou, these are questions collegians are asking today. Who am I?

* From "20th Century Blues," by Noel Coward. Copyright © 1931 by Chappell & Co., Ltd. Chappell & Co., Inc., owner of publication and allied rights for the Western Hemisphere. Used by permission.

And if there is a God, why isn't He more discoverable? Indeed, some have taken the next step and pondered the relevance of the questions themselves.

When this manuscript was still in its early stages, an East Coast campus pastor was queried about the devotional life of Christian college students. "What devotional life?" he shot back. "The first thing to say about that subject is that there isn't any!"

Why then a book of meditations for collegians? We submit that there are still many students who are willing, like the Prodigal Son, to leave the barnyard and go back to the Waiting Father. There are still those who have not committed themselves to the dogmatisms of relativism, rationalism, empiricism, or the "new humanism" and in confronting Christ-men and Christ-women on campus are willing to "search the Scriptures" to see whether these things are so. There are still students who will grant that it is not the Shepherd who is lost but the sheep — and are open-minded enough to make a systematic examination of the Christian faith and its relevance for their lives.

In a word, it is our contention that God *is* a "discoverable God," that He is a "contemporary God," that He is the God manifest in Jesus Christ, who "is before all things" and in whom "all things hold together."

To that end this little volume is offered, not so much as "devotions" but as grist for meditative reading and study. It is our hope that these vignettes will be the catalysts for directing Joe and Mary College back to the Gospels themselves, where they will find God's answer to the question Who am I? For there they will discover the person whom they are to become, and the One who is the Power to be such a "new creation" — our blessed Lord Himself.

So, "come, let us reason together."

Scripture passages are from the Revised Standard Version of the Bible unless otherwise noted. KJV designates King James Version.

Many people in the church used to think of the task of the church as "following its college students to the campus." Such phrases were used as "taking Christ to the university." This type of thinking was consonant with the idea that the college or university was somehow antichristian or unchristian by its very nature; and this further gave rise to many antiintellectual, anti-higher-education, and obscurantist views in the church.

Happily, in recent years many in the church have realized how erroneous this kind of thinking was. We now realize that Christ is on campus; in fact He has been there all the time.

First of all, Christ is on campus because all the academic disciplines and subjects which treat the nature of the world and man in it are actually concerned with *God's* world — it is His creation. And bit by bit whatever research is conducted, whatever discoveries are made are "breakthroughs" that God is permitting man to make as he plumbs deeper and deeper into the mysteries and wonders of God's vast created cosmogony. One might well ask, What has God been doing in the sciences these days?

Further, Christ is on campus, for He walks to and fro every day on the campus paths and up and down the halls of the classroom buildings, in the hearts and lives of the Christ-men and Christ-women who bear His name. They are His witnesses — "little Christs," "other Christs." And wherever they go, Christ goes and makes His call and challenge and claim on other students who still do not know Him.

Among non-Christian students the sentiment is often found that truth is somehow "on campus," in the empirical and scientific approach to subject matter. The student chapels and student centers are off-campus, are viewed as doctrinaire, and whatever good they may produce is substandard to the "truth" which is found in the high halls of learning.

The concept, of course, is erroneous; it is a dogmatism all of its own making. But there is a grain of truth in the idea too — for truth *is* on campus, because whatever is discovered is God's truth already. He is the Author and the Finisher of everything. "For in Him all things were created, in heaven and on earth, visible and invisible, whether thrones or dominions or principalities or authorities — all things were created through Him and for Him. He is before all things, and in Him all things hold together." (Colossians 1:16, 17)

So let us celebrate His presence on campus!

M any students will start a school year making many kinds of promises, but their high ideals and hopes and plans for the year quickly diminish as the school year progresses.

Many Christian students may flex their spiritual muscles at the beginning of the school year, show an immediate interest in the worship services and activities at a campus church, but the interest is short-lived, and the student soon falls back into the old ways. They were only "opening exercises."

In a number of ways the Scripture notes the need for regular, consistent, and continual exercise in the spiritual life of the child of God.

Speaking of the need of constant self-examination, the apostle Paul said: "And herein do I exercise myself, to have always a conscience void of offense toward God and toward men." (Acts 24:16 KJV)

Paul wrote to the young preacher Timothy and told him: "But refuse profane and old wives' fables, and exercise thyself rather unto godliness. For bodily exercise profiteth little; but godliness is profitable unto all things, having promise of the life that now is and of that which is to come." (1 Timothy 4:7, 8 KJV)

And speaking of the tribulation through which a Christian must go as God tests and deepens his faith and his relationship with Him, the writer to the Hebrews said: "Now no chastening for the present seemeth to be joyous, but grievous. Nevertheless, afterward it yieldeth the peaceable fruit of righteousness unto them which are exercised thereby." (Hebrews 12:11 KJV)

How about your spiritual muscles? Are they in use now, or are they atrophying?

One of the commonly debated topics on a college campus is whether Christ really was God. Many students are willing to accept Christ as a great philosopher, a profound teacher, a noble martyr who died for His principles; but they are not willing to accept Him as "God manifest in the flesh."

In speaking of the Holy Trinity we usually ascribe the work of creation to God the Father, the work of redemption to God the Son, and the work of sanctification — cleansing our hearts and bringing us into God's church through conversion — to the Holy Ghost. But as we say in the Athanasian Creed: "And yet they are not three Gods but one God. So likewise the Father is Lord, the Son Lord, and the Holy Ghost Lord. And yet not three Lords, but one Lord."

And witness to this consonance of the three Persons of the Trinity in one God is found in Paul's letter to the Colossian Christians, where Paul notes how we should give thanks unto the Father, "who hath delivered us from the power of darkness and hath translated us into the kingdom of His dear Son, in whom we have redemption through His blood, even the forgiveness of sins." And then, speaking of the Second Person of the Trinity, Paul says: "Who is the Image of the invisible God, the Firstborn of every creature; for by Him were all things created that are in heaven and that are in earth, visible and invisible, whether they be thrones or dominions or principalities or powers: all things were created by Him and for Him; and He is before all things, and by Him all things consist" (Colossians 1:12-17 KJV). The RSV neatly translates this: "In Him all things hold together."

Indeed, Christ is God! He is the Creator of all the universes.

Deep in the heart of Africa a safari ground to a halt one afternoon when the natives refused to go any farther. The leaders of the expedition went back to where they were lying on the grass, exhausted, and asked them what was wrong. The answer came that they had to "wait awhile to let their souls catch up with their bodies." For them the life principle was associated with their breath, and it was coming in gasps too short to let their bodies go any farther.

Who has not at some time felt spiritually empty, drained of any resources to continue a vigorous and dynamic life in Christ on campus? God made us as beings who need rest. But even more than physical rest, there is the spiritual need to "come apart and rest awhile."

Christ invites us to a quiet hour when we will get our power from Him. "Come to Me, all who labor and are heavy laden, and I will give you rest. Take My yoke upon you, and learn from Me; for I am gentle and lowly in heart, and you will find rest for your souls. For My yoke is easy, and My burden is light." (Matthew 11:28-30)

He invites us to rest and meditate — to relive our Christian Baptism, where we were buried with Christ "by Baptism into death, so that as Christ was raised from the dead by the glory of the Father, we too might walk in newness of life" (Romans 6:4). This newness of life is also ours in the Lord's Supper, where we receive the food of God's own love and forgiveness. Here too we have the gracious invitation: "Ho, everyone who thirsts, come to the waters; and he who has no money, come, buy and eat! Come, buy wine and milk without money and without price." (Isaiah 55:1)

Time out! "Rest in the Lord, and wait patiently for Him." (Psalm 37:7 KJV)

Several students were walking across the quadrangle of a large university just as the bell tower chimed five o'clock in the afternoon. At that precise moment in front of them on the sidewalk a foreign student dropped full length on the ground to the utter amazement of those walking behind him. After the initial shock the students realized that he had not stumbled or fallen but was a Moslem who was prostrating himself at his holy hour of prayer.

That man was not ashamed of his religion. How many of us are not ashamed to make known that we are Christians: through prayer before meals in the campus cafeteria, before studying in the library, or upon beginning that heavy examination in the classroom?

How many of us by omission of prayer, or other practices that might designate that we are Christians, in effect become guilty of the sin of the apostle Peter when he said: "I do not know the Man"? (Matthew 26:74). What a tragedy for those who have been nominal members of the church, but about whom Christ will one day say: "And then will I declare to them, 'I never knew you' "! (Matthew 7:23)

The positive injunction of Scripture is: "Let your light so shine before men that they may see your good works and give glory to your Father who is in heaven" (Matthew 5:16). We are to be "blameless and innocent, children of God without blemish in the midst of a crooked and perverse generation, among whom you shine as lights in the world." (Philippians 2:15)

Therefore let us say with the apostle Paul: "I am not ashamed of the Gospel: it is the power of God for salvation to everyone who has faith." (Romans 1:16)

It had been a long vigil during those last few months. The campus pastor and his parishioner had sat by the bedside of the young man's wife. She had terminal cancer. But the time finally came when the phone rang at the parsonage a little after midnight and he heard the words at the other end of the line: "Pastor, she's gone."

All the resources of medical research had been drained to try to save this young woman's life, but to no avail — another life was over. Help for this young woman, both human and technological, stopped at death's door.

God has permitted man to discover many things in the various sciences. And the Christian student sees all research and the use of the scientific method as God's own gift to Him. But at the same time he recognizes the limitations, the definitive limitations of these tools. Even if and when scientists synthetically "create" life (and it appears this is just a matter of time), the question will still remain as to the Author behind "life," matter, and energy in the first place.

For the Christian student it is not a question. For him the whole of Scripture and the whole of life is stamped with those mighty first four words of the Book of Genesis: "In the beginning God." "From Him and through Him and to Him are all things" (Romans 11:36). And ultimately beyond all that God has permitted us to discover about man and the world in which he lives, it is our majestic Creator-God with whom we have to deal.

Truly, "He did not leave Himself without witness" (Acts 14:17). But God's majesty is evident not only in all the wonders of this creation but also in coming to us in the form of His beloved Son. It is in Him that we find the purpose of all the universes — and of our own lives.

James A. Pike edited the book *Modern Canterbury Pilgrims,* which consists of a number of essays by prominent men who describe why they chose the Episcopal Church. One of them, John H. Hallowell, tells how he was first attracted to Christianity once he was shown that it was intellectually relevant to the problems with which he was professionally concerned.

But long before this in the course of his academic career other men had had a profoundly negative influence on him in contributing to the demolition of whatever Christian faith he had as a youth. He recalls one man: "But my genial professor, a true skeptic to the last, closed the course as he began it, with a quizzical smile, and while I came away admiring his dialectical skill, I also came away with a sense of the intellectual futility of seeking answers to the most basic questions."

Happily, most Christians have dispensed with the practice of characterizing professors on a secular college campus as atheistic ogres who are trying to destroy the faith of gullible freshmen. Many of these men, even though they are not Christians, are honestly seeking to get their students to "think for themselves." And the process of challenge can be a very fruitful one for the Christian student who goes to God's resources for the strengthening and rebuilding of his faith at this critical period of his life.

But it is always good to keep in mind the question: Is the professor at this point dealing solely with the facts of the case, or is he now putting his own mental construct on things? Is he being true to his own discipline, or has he stepped out of his field to make comments on his own?

Even as in doctrinal and spiritual matters the Christian

student does not believe every spirit but tests the spirits "to see whether they are of God" (1 John 4:1), so in the academic world he will listen critically to whatever presentations are made. He will be aware of the purely "human point of view" that can enter into his professor's statements; but he will also welcome the testing and the challenge which the professor's confrontation provides him.

Did you ever think of the Holy Communion service as a drama? It is — high drama.

In fact, this play with its characters, its gripping plot, and theme has been playing to packed houses for 20 centuries. The story is almost melodramatic. It is the story of a lost child, a child who has rejected everything that his father has done for him. But it is also a story of *rapprochement,* of reconciliation between the erring child and the loving, forgiving father.

It is, of course, the drama of salvation — of man's salvation. The one place where the analogy does not hold is in that we were not spectators to this great reenactment of the history of man's relationship with God as it is played out on the stage before us in the chancel. No, we are not observers; we are all a key character — the erring prodigal who has run away from the family of God.

Isaiah's words apply to us: "Your iniquities have made a separation between you and your God, and your sins have hid His face from you so that He does not hear" (Isaiah 59: 2). So we must say with David: "Against Thee, Thee only have I sinned and done that which is evil in Thy sight." (Psalm 51:4)

Then we will also share in the end of the drama. It is the story told in so many beautiful ways in Luke 15: The one lost sheep is found by the shepherd, and he rejoices; the one lost coin is found after a diligent search, and the woman rejoices with her neighbors; and the prodigal son returns to the waiting father, who says: "We'll have to have a celebration. I thought my son was dead, and he is alive; I thought he was lost, and he is found!"

Let's say it again: "What a wonderful God we have!"

Sandwiches and Buttermilk

A student at the University of Michigan was working on his master's thesis on remedial techniques for stutterers. He was a stutterer himself, and one day he received an unusual assignment from his professor in the speech clinic. He was to go into a local jewerly store and with a poker face say, "I would like some sandwiches and buttermilk, please."

The clerk in the store, of course, would look at him with blank amazement, probably wondering to himself, "What kind of a nut do I have here?"

But the student was to follow through with the experiment, ending the encounter with: "Well, at least could you tell me where I could find some?" He would then thank the gentleman as he left. The point of the whole process was to get the stutterers used to the strange looks that people would give them when they were standing in a group, would try to talk, and instead begin to stutter.

It may not be stretching the analogy too far to compare this with the response of many non-Christians to the attitudes, the feelings, and the statements of Christian men and women. To illustrate: A seminary professor once remarked, "Think of the reaction of a psychiatrist if he were to have a chance conversation with a man he did not know was a pastor, and he asked him, 'By the way, what do you do?' And to this the pastor would reply, 'Oh, I forgive sins every week.'"

The Christian student who lives out a life of integrity and consistent practicing of his faith on a college campus cannot expect to be liked by everyone. "It's your virtues that make your enemies but your vices that make your friends." That's the way the old saying goes. And people are not going to want someone around who reminds them of the person that they should be, indeed, could be with Christ at the center of their life.

Further, the world not only rejects, it persecutes those who live the Christ life. It nailed the Source of this life to a cross many years ago. The rationale of the world's response is found in John 15:18, 19: "If the world hates you, know that it has hated Me before it hated you. If you were of the world, the world would love its own; but because you are not of the world, but I chose you out of the world, therefore the world hates you."

The Christian student may lose some friends through the full-scale living out of his Christian faith; but he still has the most important Friend of all — the Friend of sinners.

"I was shocked!" said the student. "Here I'd been home for two weeks for Christmas vacation, and somehow, to my amazement, I just didn't use any of the foul words that I had grown to use all during the fall semester here at school. There just didn't seem to be any occasion to use them. Maybe it's that I didn't have anybody that I felt I had to impress by letting go with a blue phrase or two.

"But, you know, within a matter of hours when I got back to campus, I caught myself saying some of the dirtiest words I have ever used. I don't know what got into me! Back in this setting — where there are kids who do the same thing all the time — it was so easy to lose control of my tongue. I really felt ashamed of myself."

The old proverb goes: "Birds of a feather flock together." Even the Christian student is often surprised to find that there is so much residual evil in him from the old Adam that he can very easily fall into vices in new surroundings which he may have been overcoming in a stronger, more Christian atmosphere. This is why the choice of friends is such a crucial point. We are like sensitive radar screens, always being influenced by other people for good or ill, even as we influence them for good or ill.

We may think that those whose language or morals or activities are unchristian may not influence us very much, that we have a strong faith and will be able to overcome any temptation. But "can a man carry fire in his bosom and his clothes not be burned? Or can one walk upon hot coals and his feet not be scorched?" (Proverbs 6:27, 28)

As a man "thinketh in his heart, so is he" (Proverbs 23:7 KJV). And since Satan can work 24 hours a day on our mind and conscience, seeking to lead us away from God's path, it is vital that we think the right things and have as our closest friends those who are members of the body of Christ. (This is not to say that the Christian absents himself from friendship with non-Christians, for otherwise how could he witness to them? The point is, one is not to be unaware of the influence for evil which can be brought to bear on one's faith and life.)

The spiritual food of the Christian therefore, the friends, the fellowship — all these will dictate whether the heart that lies behind the tongue will produce the right fruit. When his food and speech are the precious Gospel of Jesus Christ, then he is on the road to being the master of his tongue. For this Gospel enables him to say with the psalmist: "The precepts of the Lord are right, rejoicing the heart; the commandment of the Lord is pure, enlightening the eyes. . . . Let the words of my mouth and the meditation of my heart be acceptable in Thy sight, O Lord, my Rock and my Redeemer." (Psalm 19:8, 14)

"Keep thyself pure," urges the Scripture. "Whatever is true, whatever is honorable, whatever is just, whatever is pure, whatever is lovely, whatever is gracious, if there is any excellence, if there is anything worthy of praise, think about these things." (Philippians 4:8)

For an assignment in an educational psychology course a young Christian student once prepared a list of questions which he passed around in a dormitory to get the ideas of various students on religion. One of the sheets was returned to him with none of the blanks marked or filled out in any way but with the irate note scribbled at the top of the page, "I've never read so many predicated and narrow-minded questions!"

This is a common reaction to Christians and to Christianity on the part of many people. "Narrow-minded!" is the cry. "Why do you Christians have to be so exasperatingly exclusive? Why do you have to think that your religion is the only true religion? Why do you say that your view of Christ is the right one?"

The "exclusiveness" and "narrow-mindedness" is not that of the Christians themselves but rather of Christ Himself. The Scriptural record is clear. Read it for yourself: "And there is salvation in no one else, for there is no other name under heaven given among men by which we must be saved" (Acts 4:12). The context speaks of "the name of Jesus Christ of Nazareth, whom you crucified, whom God raised from the dead" (Acts 4:10). This is the only name that we can bear: Christ-men and Christ-women, if we would enter the gates of heaven in the family of God.

Christ Himself said: "Unless you repent, you will all . . . perish" (Luke 13:3). He told Nicodemus: "Truly, truly I say to you, unless one is born anew, he cannot see the kingdom of God." (John 3:3)

But the promise is clear: "Whoever confesses that Jesus is the Son of God, God abides in him and he in God." (1 John 4:15)

Ping-pong balls were ricocheting downstairs in the basement of the student center, but this student pulled the campus pastor aside upstairs and said, "I've just got to talk to you. Pastor, you tell us to witness to our Christian faith, but you don't tell us how to do it."

The young man had a good point. We often know what we are supposed to do, but we don't know just how to do it. On the other hand, we can overemphasize the how of witnessing to the Gospel and the various methods of reaching people with its precious message of the forgiveness of sins.

A promise to some of the early disciples was that God would put into their lips the words they needed to say when the time and the place occurred. We may not all have the same gifts they had, but we certainly still have the same promise of power from the same beneficent and all-wise God.

If a Christian student has a firm grounding in his own life, if he is making use of the Scriptures and Holy Communion regularly and penitently, to a great extent he is going to know what to say and when to say it. All of this is not to say that there will be some kind of mechanical, automatic response. But one who is immersed in the sea of God's love, one who is plugged into the source of power which is Christ, will be moved to "speak of the things that he has seen and heard."

A careful study of the processes of communication and the dynamics of dialog is vital to a faithful witness on the college campus. But the most important preparation for the presentation of the Christian Gospel is to be fully "in Christ," then go in confidence that the promise of God stands sure: "Fear not, for I am with you; be not dismayed, for I am your God; I will strengthen you, I will help you, I will uphold you with My victorious right hand." (Isaiah 41:10)

Students at some universities may turn in self-addressed postcards with their final examination papers; thus they need not wait long to learn what their final grades are. One fellow always glued four-leaf clovers to his cards, with the comment, "Usually it helps."

I remember seeing one student's postcard after it had been returned; on it the reader had scribbled in red pencil, "A — by the skin of your teeth."

Some people would like to get to heaven if only "by the skin of their teeth." But there is some horribly warped thinking in this conception of Christianity.

For one thing, in the final analysis one doesn't "get to heaven" by anything that he does. It is totally God at work in him. And this is what many people have difficulty seeing. From outside the context of faith, "believing on the Lord Jesus Christ" looks like the deliberate choice of man's own will.

But once he has stepped through the doorway of faith, the Christian realizes the step, the very desire to return to Christ, was the blessed action of the Holy Spirit. (Nor was it against the Christian's will to resist.) And looking up through the spectacles of faith he now sees and comprehends the sign over the inside of the door: "The only way you got in here was by the grace of God."

In that sense, and in that sense alone, are we saved "by the skin of our teeth." Without the grace of God, without the crowning resurrection miracle which proves that we shall one day be raised from the dead, our faith is vain; we are "still in our sins" (1 Corinthians 15:17). But Christ did rise from the dead, our faith is not futile, and we have the certainty of lively life in God now and into all eternity.

The campus newspaper at the University of Minnesota once reported that 143 students had attended a Lutheran student meeting right in the middle of finals. The article then went on to ask: "What kind of Christians are these who will attend the meeting of a religious group at such a hectic time as finals? Could they be religious fanatics?"

It's a good question. What kind of Christians are they? Well, they are certainly interested Christians, living, doing, sharing Christians. Some people believe that today's college student is just another "4-F" — interested in little more than the four Fs of football, fame, fashions, and fraternities. But Christian students — and take those at Minnesota for an example — have much more than the four Fs to concern them. They are concerned about the problem of sin and what it is doing to men's lives. And they are making their first task on the campus the declaring of "Christ and Him crucified" to those still living without the "Lamb of God that taketh away the sin of the world."

The well-known volume *Who's Who* lists famous and great Americans. Eighty-six percent of these men and women have a college education. It is said college graduates have 800 times better chance for success than those with no education, 200 times better chance than those with only elementary education, and 10 times more chance than those with a high school education. But education should never be an end in itself. An educated mind must always be blended with a consecrated heart. And this is the balance which the Christian college student seeks to find.

What are you really doing with your life on campus? Do you have a fully balanced life, with Christ as your Foundation and your Guide?

"Students don't lose their faith in college! If this is said, they didn't have any faith when they got there."

There is a lot of truth in these statements. Even Philip E. Jacobs' famous study *Changing Values in College* bears out the fact that students do not essentially change their value structure during their academic years. The point is that the values, the beliefs, the attitudes about life have usually crystallized several years before one comes to the halls of ivy.

To this extent some of the church's work is a "salvage operation" — seeking to repair damage that has been done or seeking to implement and improve training in Christian doctrine that a student may never have properly or fully received. (This is not to exclude the crucial thrust of our campus ministry as *mission* — to one another and to those who do not know Christ.)

Look back in your own life. What kind of spiritual development did you have during the four years before you came to college? Did you read Scripture regularly, commune faithfully and penitently, live with the rich fellowship of other Christians, and grow in your knowledge of Scripture? In many cases a Christian student may still be maintaining a conception of a "little God" which has hardly kept up with his growth in other areas of knowledge and he needs to divest himself of a "hand-me-down religion" which has never really been made his very own and has not kept pace with his maturation through the developmental stages of youth.

Why not "be scientific" about it? Why not take a good look at your Christian faith again and see if it has the maturity, the depth, and the contemporaneity it should?

This will mean study of the Scriptures, it will mean discussion with other Christians, it will mean counsel with a campus pastor — a thorough and systematic investigation of Christian doctrine.

A woman who is a professor of English literature at a girls' college once invited me to speak to several of her classes on "Theology and Contemporary Literature." I made the point that even as we do not "read into" Hemingway a view that is not really his own in the book, so we should come to the Scriptures with an open mind and let it speak to us from within itself. The woman was amazed at the insight — a principle which she actually had been trying to get across to her students all year long as they studied various works of literature. She said, "You know, I think I'm going to go back and read the Bible all over again, keeping in mind that principle that you suggested."

Try it! Just how mature is your faith?

It can be a challenging and exhilarating adventure as you discover all over again the depth, the height, the length, and the breadth of the Christian faith in your own life and a God who is more contemporary than you have ever realized He could be. And you too can be amazed at what the grace and gift of God in Christ can do in you as God rebuilds your faith.

In many areas of the church in the past there has been the pervading notion that "politics is dirty business." And so some Christians have not involved themselves in this necessary aspect of national life, yes, also of campus life — voting in student elections, running for campus office, or serving the student body in some other similar way.

But we must distinguish between the field of politics and some of the individuals who have given it a negative aura. Since the Christian student is on campus to serve to the extent that his studies will permit, he should seriously consider his obligation — if God has given him the talents — to become involved in campus politics.

One campus pastor put it this way: "Certainly I would like to see that gifted student active in my student organization here at the campus chapel — we could certainly use his leadership abilities in our group! But I am also concerned that our students be involved in campus life and make their witness whenever and wherever they can. For the Christian student 'witnesses where he is,' and effecting a better campus life for the whole academic community by becoming involved in campus politics in my book is just as necessary and worthy a calling as being an officer in a student-church organization."

The Christian student is in but not of the campus world. That is, he does not simply reflect the values on campus but becomes a fruitful stimulant for the values which would be pleasing to God.

True, the Christian student is to "keep himself unstained from the world" (James 1:27), but he must also get out of his churchly ghetto and serve and work and live with men, for by so doing he is serving Christ. And he is serving as Christ served.

There is a lot of truth in the old saying, "Don't tell me what you are, because what you do speaks so loudly."

We all do judge a person by what he does, not just by what he says. "Deeds, not creeds," is a phrase that has a world of meaning in it, properly understood.

Many people outside the church have refused to step into its fellowship because of the inconsistencies and contradictions which they have noted in the lives of those who claim to be "good Christians." And yet the point should be made that the church — like any group within society — has its "weak sisters." Man, not being a puppet, has freedom to act at great variance from what he should be.

Although the hypocrites and weak Christians who are obvious to outsiders are a stumbling block to others in becoming members of Christ's fellowship, the ultimate question still remains: What are you doing with Christ and His claim on your life? A little tract by the Inter-Varsity Christian Fellowship is titled "Have You Considered Him?" It deals with a thorough treatment of the person, work, and life of Christ — who He was and what He claimed about Himself. In the final analysis, all the weak Christians in the world cannot be an excuse for a person's not coming to terms with this great God-man who stands at the very turning point of history.

A Christian is really a signpost pointing to Christ. He says, "Don't just look at me and my life. I may be a poor witness at times to the Christian faith, but I am striving every day by God's grace to do better. I urge you to look at Him who has given me forgiveness for my sins and constantly calls me and alone gives me power to be a better self. You belong to this Christ. What are you doing with Him?"

In his incisive novel *The Fall* Albert Camus gives a penetrating description of a man who is in love with himself. The protagonist, John Baptiste Clemence, is obsessed by an overwhelming self-love and by a constant drive to dominate and use and manipulate other people. He speaks of "keeping them in the refrigerator" so that he can bring them out whenever he wants to make use of them for his own ends and purposes.

This is a besetting problem for all of us — Christians too, who are still plagued by the presence of the old man in their hearts. We are so often prone to use other people as means rather than as ends. We like to manipulate them to serve our own purposes and desires rather than to see these people as ends in themselves to be served and helped and loved. To dominate and manipulate other people, to see them only as tools by which we get what we want, is really a horrible thing. In one sense it is a form of prostitution. It makes of a person only a thing. It denigrates human personality and destroys the worth that God has placed into every human being. Christ came not to be served but to serve. It is our calling to determine how we can help others, not just "use them" to help us get what we want.

Look around. Who is there that you have been climbing over and using as a tool to get to the top of some goal that you have set for yourself?

"Neither be called masters, for you have one Master, the Christ. He who is greatest among you shall be your servant" (Matthew 23:10, 11). "For to this you have been called, because Christ suffered for you, leaving you an example, that you should follow in His steps." (1 Peter 2:21)

There was an earnest and puzzled look on the co-ed's face. She had been recently confirmed and with God's help had sought to lead a true and consistent Christian life. But one thing disturbed her.

"Pastor, I know that you're not supposed to hate anybody," she began. "But is it alright if you just can't stand someone?"

It was Will Rogers who once said, "I never met a man I didn't like." Perhaps not all of us could say that as we look back upon everybody with whom we have come in contact during our lives, especially on campus, where the pressures and exigencies of the academic routine often bring very different personalities into conflict. Indeed, there is even Scriptural support for the fact that not everybody's personality is going to mesh perfectly with our own. Throughout the Old and New Testament there are numerous instances of people who radically disagreed with each other and sometimes came to a parting of the ways because they simply could not work together in harmony.

But the Scripture has a positive insight on this business of different personalities. It calls this "the difference of gifts." Paul told the Roman Christians that there were "gifts that differ according to the grace given to us" (Romans 12:6). In Ephesians 4 he lists the different roles that people play in the church of God. And in writing to the Galatian Christians he describes how he "opposed" Peter to his face because he was to be blamed for not having fellowship with some of the new Gentile Christians. (Galatians 2:11, 12)

So although there may be extremely different personalities, characters, and gifts among us — and because of this there are bound to be problems of misunderstanding even within the church — the glory of our fellowship is that although there are "varieties of gifts" we have "the same Spirit" (1 Corinthians 12:4). In the context of this chapter the apostle demonstrates how much we all need one another, how we suffer with one another, how we share in one another's joys and sorrows. You see, we are "one in spirit," for by the Holy Spirit we have been made one in Christ, who is the Head of all of these different members of His body.

Yes, you can be "different" in the church, for it is a difference God has given. But you are bound into a unity with all other Christians by the Christ who makes it possible to find completeness in the midst of all of our differences.

The Ugliest Man

On some college campuses there is an annual contest for "the ugliest man on campus." It is a dubious honor, but it is all in good fun. Often the young man who wins the prize is really quite a good Joe at heart and is well liked by everyone, but he hasn't been blessed with the physiognomy of some of his fellows.

There is another "ugly man" who haunts the modern college campus. He is the "Christ figure" in between the lines of some great literature. He is the carpenter's Son whose spirit still roams the streets and bypaths of the world, who still walks along the campus mall, and who bids man to "come after Him and follow Him."

Isaiah wrote: "He had no form or comeliness that we should look at Him, and no beauty that we should desire Him" (Isaiah 53:2). Not speaking of Christ's physical appearance, of course, the appearance of Christ to His children and His claim as Lord of their lives does not meet with a warm response in the heart of natural man. For the Scripture says: "He was despised and rejected by men, a man of sorrows and acquainted with grief; and as one from whom men hide their faces He was despised, and we esteemed Him not." (Isaiah 53:3)

Here is the Great Embarrassment, the Great Stumbling Block, the Scandal of Christianity incarnate in the Son of Man, who dies on a cursed cross and claims that He is the Savior of all the world. Here is "a Stone that will make men stumble, a Rock that will make them fall" (1 Peter 2:8) — literally, many people "just can't get over it" — this Christ and His cross.

Oh, of course, there are those students who will say that they "like Christ and His teachings," that they are not "against Christ." But they aren't really speaking of the Christ of the Gospels, whose call is a hard one. They are thinking of only His ethical teachings, not "repentance for the forgiveness of sins." For Christ makes claim upon man's whole life and says: "He who is not with Me is against Me" (Matthew 12:30) — not Me the great teacher, the great philosopher, the ethical culturalist, but Me "the Son of Man, who has come to seek and to save that which was lost."

This is a total claim, a claim of judgment upon our sins and a claim for service in the totality of our lives. But when we have been faithful in confessing our sins, we find that Christ's totalitarian control over us has given us perfect freedom! For the "Ugly Man" is also the answer to all the ugliness in our own lives, our Savior for this life and the life which is to come.

Did you ever take a course in which you wondered where in the world the professor was going? There just didn't seem to be any rhyme or reason in his conduct of the course.

I once had such a course in sociology. It was about the driest and dullest thing I had ever sat through. Nevertheless, I faithfully took notes throughout the semester and worked hard just on the principle of the thing, hoping I would ultimately get something out of it. To my utter amazement about six months later I used much of the structure of the course and the principles I had learned in it for a major piece of graduate work.

Houston Peterson in *Great Teachers* notes that when some lecturers finish what they have been talking about, the conclusions are there; they have been neatly measured and packaged, and everybody feels pleased. But nobody cares to come back to the subject again.

In contrast to such teachers he noted those who come to grips with real problems and are not too systematic in their presentation; when they finsh their lecture, there are a lot of "loose ends," but they are "live ends," and you can do something with them.

Our Christian lives are often this way too. They are not neatly packaged with all problems solved and all answers given to all the questions that we raise about the whys of life. We are plagued by tensions of many kinds in our campus life — worrying about being accepted by other people, worrying about the term paper or the assignment that is almost due, worrying about whether we will meet expenses for the year.

But above and behind the whole campus scene there is One who knows everything that is going on in our lives.

He is not pulling puppet strings but is letting us pass through the tests and trials of life that we might better realize our need and dependency on Him.

We hear someone speak of "God's plan for your life" and decide that it is certainly a nonsystematic job so far as our lives are concerned. But God has given us some "live ends" by which we might find the direction for our lives and know that He is still in control of all that lies ahead.

These live ends are the life-giving forgiveness of sins found in His precious Word, in the renewal of our baptismal vow each day, and in the regular, penitent use of the Lord's Supper. When we have these reins in our hands, we can know right where we are going, even though we can't see the final destination clearly.

J. B. Phillips put it this way in his paraphrase of Romans 12:2: "Let God remold your minds from within, so that you may prove in practice that the plan of God for you is good, meets all His demands, and moves toward the goal of true maturity."

James D. Smart in his excellent educational text, *The Teaching Ministry of the Church,* tells of a group of high school teachers who were asked to teach a new curriculum in the youth department of their church. The course was titled "Christ and Humanism." It included noting distinctions between such approaches as Dale Carnegie's *How to Win Friends and Influence People* and the teachings of Christ in the New Testament.

After studying the materials, these teachers refused to teach the course, saying that they saw no valid distinction or contradiction between Christianity and humanism. To them Dale Carnegie and Christ were "just good companions," and Christianity and humanism were "inextricably intermingled."

Here was a tragic case of people who had nominally grown up as Christians, but their approach to life was that of humanism — that "man is the measure of all things."

Is man the measure? Second Corinthians 10 has something to say about this. It speaks of "casting down imaginations and every high thing that exalteth itself against the knowledge of God, and bringing into captivity every thought to the obedience of Christ" (2 Corinthians 10:5 KJV). Paul goes on to say that the only "measure" that man really has is the rule which God has set for us. "He that glorieth, let him glory in the Lord. For not he that commendeth himself is approved, but whom the Lord commendeth." (2 Corinthians 10:17, 18 KJV)

Man is not the measure of all things, but God is the Great Measurer. "It is He that made us and not we ourselves." His measure of man reads: "There is not a righteous man on earth who does good and never sins" (Ecclesiastes 7:20). Humanism radically rejects this, saying that man is essentially good and has within himself the power to overcome the problems that face mankind.

But "there is no difference, for all have sinned and come short of the glory of God, being justified freely by His grace through the redemption that is in Christ Jesus" (Romans 3:22-24 KJV). Thank God, there is a measure for all of us who have come short of God's rule — He is the greatest "human" of them all, but also the Son of God and the Savior of the world. In Him alone is our only real hope.

Yes, there is a difference!

At the end of his first pastoral letter to the young preacher Timothy the apostle Paul said: "O Timothy, guard what has been entrusted to you. Avoid the godless chatter and contradictions of what is falsely called knowledge, or by professing it some have missed the mark as regards the faith. Grace be with you." (1 Timothy 6:20, 21)

At first sight this charge to Timothy gives the impression that his job was mostly to be one of guarding and preserving his faith. But no passage of the Bible is to be seen in isolation from the others, and Paul had much to say in both this letter and his next one to Timothy with respect to an active, dynamic, growing, and vital faith. For being a Christian is not just a matter of avoiding false philosophies but of building on the foundation which already is ours through faith in Jesus Christ.

Our faith in our Lord is no academic trophy to be put into some display case and hermetically sealed, untouched, until some great day. Rather it is a faith to be quickened and nurtured and developed. To be a Christian at all we must (in Paul's own words to Timothy) "stir up the gift of God which is in us" — through study of Scripture and worship, reception of the Blessed Sacrament, and prayer; for one cannot be a Christian in a vacuum.

And when, as growing Christians in a culture which is a challenge to our faith, we let God do His gracious work in us this way, then we are not "missing the mark" as so many do. For to "hit the mark" is to be centered on our Lord Jesus Christ, who loved us and came among us and suffered and died for us, who rose again and has entrusted to us that Christian faith which is our eternal union with Him.

Some critics of the modern university have accused it of academic schizophrenia and dubbed it the "multiversity." The contemporary seat of learning is no longer the university of the 13th century, where theology was queen and the very etymology of the word was true: *univertere* — to combine together into one.

Rather, today's school has many different departments and disciplines, unrelated to religion and often as quite separate entities unto themselves. One person said that the only thing that connects the various departments on his campus is the plumbing.

Nevertheless, as the church looks at the fragmented state of much secular college and university education today, it does not "sit across the moat and throw rocks at the university." Rather it engages in dialog with the university that both churchman and educator may together take into account the whole man who is being educated.

Church and university — both have their role to play in the maturation of Joe and Mary College. The secular university does not exist to give the collegian one specific *Weltanschauung* or religious faith. But it should posit the need for a philosophy of life, for an integrating principle for the multiplicity of studies which the student undertakes.

Church and university are therefore partners in the educational enterprise. And the student benefits from the resources of each, the rational and the spiritual, the natural and the eternal.

Church and university. They are both gifts of God to man. And for the benefits which come from each the renewed Christian praises and thanks God, "from whom all blessings flow."

A certain exchange student had been a Christian for only a few years. After a brief period of study and visiting in the United States she and her husband returned to her homeland. Not long afterward her husband died suddenly.

In writing to a friend in America, commenting on the death, this fledgling Christian puzzled over why God had let him die, but the letter carried no bitterness or complaint. Instead she wrote: "Christ never, never leave me down. My eyes are full of tears with happiness, remembering *small* treasures. I'll never stop singing songs to praise my Christ Child. Lord makes me brave. I take Bible everywhere and do not hesitate to sing and pray among non-Christian friends. I cannot die, because Christ insists me to live and to work for His glory. I am His slave."

What a testimony of faith! We often speak of having a "mission" to people in foreign lands. But when one looks at the apathy in many of our churches, in the lives of many of our people, and then hears a testimony of faith like this, one is tempted to say that these young Christians and young churches in other lands have a mission to *us*. Maybe they can bring us back to the original fire and burning enthusiasm of faith which it so often seems we have lost.

Let us pray with the hymn writer:

> Send Thou, O Lord, to every place
> Swift messengers before Thy face,
> The heralds of Thy wondrous grace,
> Where Thou Thyself wilt come.
>
> Send men whose eyes have seen the King,
> Men in whose ears His sweet words ring . . .

People often have a way of inverting things from the way they really are. There is the old story of the college student who asked another what he was doing. The other replied, "Oh, I'm searching for God." To this the first said, "Oh, is He lost again?"

This is an all too frequent reversal of the parable of Christ as the Good Shepherd. The problem is that man thinks he is searching for God, whereas it is really man who is lost and the Good Shepherd has come to seek and to save him.

Or take the very relationship that each of us has in faith through Christ. We may often think that the question is: Does God really love me? Or we may think: Can I learn to love other people? The real question is: Am I going to let Christ help me with His love?

Christ said: "Him that cometh to Me I will in no wise cast out" (John 6:37 KJV). Recall the great Gospel promise in the Old Testament: "Fear not, for I am with you; be not dismayed, for I am your God; I will strengthen you, I will help you, I will uphold you with My victorious right hand." (Isaiah 41:10)

Truly, this is the God who can turn our lives upside down and put things back into their proper perspective when we have put things into disorder and chaos. May we, as the apostles and evangelists were described in Acts 17:6, also be "men who have turned the world upside down" as we help those around us find the true balance and perspective in life and work.

READ JOHN 10

John Dewey used to say that the only thing that we can be certain of is change itself.

Many things certainly have changed in the world's history. Man's conception of his universe has changed from his being awed with the earth on which he walked to looking at the universe of planets around him to finally realizing that it was not a universe but rather millions of universes extending far beyond the mind's comprehension.

There has also been much change in terms of man's attempts to live in the strange, new world which has been foisted upon him; and many writers have spoken of the different kinds of "man" which are needed to fill the gap between where we are now and where scientific exploration will take us in the future.

We quite often forget, however, to examine the facets of the "new man" of whom the New Testament speaks and who the Christian church holds is the only answer to meet the problems of this new age.

This is the new man we become through faith in our Lord and Savior Jesus Christ. He is at once God's revelation to us of the persons we are to be, and the transforming power to become such new individuals. It is true, our cosmology has changed, our culture has shifted, our verbal symbols and media of communication have been transposed. But sinful men are still the same today, and our God is still the same. The truth still remains, the challenge to each one of us: "Put on the new man, which after God is created in righteousness and true holiness" (Ephesians 4:23 KJV). Only then is man — the Christian man — prepared to live in a strange, new world.

The black-haired co-ed had been sitting in the pastor's study for about an hour, complaining bitterly about the treatment other members in the choir had been giving her. Finally, after a long pause, the girl looked up and said quietly, "But this isn't my real problem, Pastor. My real difficulty is that I have been sleeping with my fiancé, and I just had to talk to you about it."

Then the real counseling began. The pastor assured the girl of God's forgiveness if there was true penitence on her part for what she had been doing. He went on to demonstrate the difference between God's forgiveness and forgiveness as many human beings think of it, for they may often say, "Oh, sure, I forgive you, but I don't see how I can forget about it!" This is in sharp contrast to God's forgiveness, which is really a full pardon. A pardon does not mean that a crime was never committed but rather that the crime and its debt have been fully accounted for and the record is now wiped clean. This is the blessed gift that is now ours because of the death of Christ on the cross for our sins.

Here are the amazing and heartwarming words of our God Himself in Isaiah 43:25: "I, I am He who blots out your transgressions for My own sake, and I will not remember your sins."

Just think, we have the kind of God who not only forgives but no longer even remembers our sins.

I believe it was O. P. Kretzmann who once made the comment that we should learn to pray something like this: "O Lord, forgive me for the sin of coming back to you and asking forgiveness for sins which you forgave and forgot a long time ago."

What a God! What a pardon!

She was working on her doctorate in chemistry, the students at the chapel remembered. And they never forgot the time she first visited the student center. She had wandered in and accosted one of the students lounging in the vestibule and said, "I am an atheist. Argue with me." To this the other student replied calmly, "Why, we don't argue with anybody around here. Come on in."

The young woman stayed for three years, even sang in the choir, but did not join the church. Nevertheless, she often admitted the strong pull of the Gospel message, which she somehow couldn't quite accept. At one time she confided to the campus pastor, "I just can't see believing in all that you do. But sometimes I still feel that God is chasing after me. The hound of heaven may get me yet."

She, of course, was referring to the famous poem by Francis Thompson, "The Hound of Heaven." For years the author himself had tried hard to escape from God. He had turned to many poor substitutes, but all in vain:

> I fled Him down the nights and down the days;
> I fled Him down the arches of the years;
> I fled Him down the labyrinthine ways
> Of my own mind; and in the mist of tears
> I hid from Him, and under running laughter.
> Up vistaed hopes I sped;
> And shot, precipitated,
> Adown titanic glooms of charmed fears,
> From those strong feet that followed, followed, after.

This is the true picture of our God, a brooding, loving, concerned God, who all down through history chased after those who ran away from Him, yes, also after you and me in so many ways in our daily lives.

Even we who have been in the church for many years can still be "hiding from God." And we need to come face to face with our Creator and honestly and open-mindedly examine the claims He makes on our lives.

We need to learn to say over and over again: "Lord, what wilt Thou have me to do?" We need to listen to the loving and concerned call of our Savior and Redeemer, the One who in His infinite love suffered and died and rose again.

He is the One who says: "Behold, I stand at the door and knock. If anyone hears My voice and opens the door, I will come in to him and eat with him, and he with Me." (Revelation 3:20)

On the bright, blue jackets of the Australian Luther Leaguers is the Latin phrase: *Non ministrari sed ministrare* — "Not to be served but to serve." It is a fitting emblem of these young people — and all young Christian people — who are dedicated to the service of Christ the King.

It is not our nature, however, to fit into this pattern. We would rather have others serve us than we serve them. And we often have a way of getting so wrapped up in our own goals and plans on campus that we lose sight of the calling to be a servant — a Christ — to others. If some achievements have been reached in our own little academic world, we may in effect say to others: "Notice the good job I've been doing on campus this year! Watch me strut my stuff! Here, let me show you my grades for the last semester."

There is a justifiable pride for work well done but not when it squeezes out our primary calling of service and love to others. Here our blessed Lord Himself gave the great example and the power by which we are to be ministers one to another: "The Son of Man came not to be ministered unto but to minister [not to be served but to serve], and to give His life a ransom for many." (Mark 10:45 KJV)

So Christ's spirit is to become ours. We are not here to have others serve us, but we are here to serve God and man. "For we are his workmanship, created in Christ Jesus for good works, which God prepared beforehand that we should walk in them." (Ephesians 2:10)

Quo vadis?

What are you doing with your life? What vocation have you chosen? Every Christian student might well consider whether God wants him to go into "professional" church work. (The term "professional" is used rather than "full-time" because every person is a "full-time" Christian.) Scrutiny should be given not only to the preaching or teaching ministry but to many other phases of missionary work, social welfare under the auspices of the church, the work of a deaconess, youth ministry, and others.

Now God may well want you to be the very best engineer, nurse, teacher, economist that you can be; and this is just as noble a calling in His eyes as is professional church service. But some students have not seriously considered such church work, because they feel personally unworthy of what in their minds is so high and holy a calling.

But those in the church who have taken up this specialized service hardly feel "worthy" themselves. Nor did they have an "ecstatic experience" in most cases but rather a growing conviction that this was what God wanted them to do with their lives. They learned to depend on Him for His promise of grace, His gift of faith, His power. They knew it was "not because of deeds done by us in righteousness but in virtue of His own mercy" (Titus 3:5) that it was possible for them to enter this specialized work.

Faith and spirituality are not qualities that we "trump up" within ourselves. The Holy Spirit alone is the One who gives us the new life and the ability to serve Him. He does that in us which we are utterly unable to do.

The young freshman's dormitory room was near the campus chapel, and I had seen him in the chapel and center quite a bit during the fall semester. Indeed, it seemed he was playing ping-pong most of the time when I wandered through the undercroft of our chapel.

However, it had been too much of a good thing, and I later learned that this student had received his first "pink slip," signifying failing grades in his courses, towards the end of November. One January morning the young man confronted me and sighed as he broke the news that he had flunked out of school. Then looking around wistfully and surveying the student center for the last time, he said: "Well, at least I accomplished one thing this semester; I improved my ping-pong game."

What a tragic waste of a young man's mind and life! Here he had been at one of the greatest universities in the world, yet he had thrown a fine career down the drain by not applying himself to his studies.

It is certainly true, as the Preacher said: "Much study is a weariness of the flesh" (Ecclesiastes 12:12). There are times when we just don't feel like studying, and as the phrase goes, "Something's got to give."

But to be a Christian student is a calling all its own. God has given us a high and holy charge to be faithful in the task of being a good student. The apostle Paul writes to Timothy: "Study to show thyself approved unto God [RSV: Do your best to present yourself to God as one approved], a workman that needeth not to be ashamed, rightly dividing the Word of truth" (2 Timothy 2:15 KJV). The text, of course, is not speaking only of studying for class but rather applies to the whole of our life, which should be dedicated to the proper conduct of our work and ministry here on earth and the use of the gifts God has given us.

In a phrase, *"Study is worship."* The exacting task of drudgery involved in studying and reading and working over term papers again and again is actually a task done to the glory of God and for the benefit of man. Here we need to learn the lesson of total dedication to our calling. A social-work professor once put it this way in describing the mental frame of mind which a social worker should take to his often discouraging task: "Acting like you don't feel" was the phrase he used.

The wonderful thing is that God has not left us alone in this calling of study and meeting our class assignments. "My grace is sufficient for thee," He has said. What greater promise does a person need for whatever task confronts him?

In one "Peanuts" comic strip one of the female small fry came to Charlie Brown and said, "Yes, sir, Charlie Brown, Abraham Lincoln was a great man. Charlie Brown, would you like to have been Abraham Lincoln?"

"Well, now, I don't think so," he replied slowly; "I am having a hard enough time being just plain old Charlie Brown."

We often have a hard time learning to accept ourselves as we are. This does not mean that we are not to improve our Christian character with God's help and make the most of such gifts as we have. But we often bring a great deal of anxiety upon ourselves because we are trying to be a person whom we can't become.

We may admire another individual whose talents far outweigh our own, and we feel terribly guilty and inferior as we compare ourselves with that individual. Or we may actually compensate by "cutting that person down to size" through malicious gossip or some other way of "giving him a bad time."

But this anxiety is needless. Scripture says: "I bid everyone among you not to think of himself more highly than he ought to think but to think with sober judgment" (Romans 12:3 KJV). This calls for real humility. It involves an appreciation and full use of the talents, gifts, and abilities that God has given one, balanced on the other hand by a recognition of the limits of personality potential with which one is endowed.

God does not expect me to be a person other than myself. But he does expect me to make a full use of my God-given abilities and to live a life of integrity and faithfulness before

Him. The question is not: How am I doing in comparison to other people? But the question is: How am I doing in comparison with God's will and standard for my life?

"It is required in stewards that a man be found faithful." (1 Corinthians 4:2 KJV)

One Christian put it this way: "When I die I will not be asked, 'Why were you not St. Paul, why were you not Luther, why were you not this or that great leader in the church?' I will be asked, 'Why were you not *you?*' "

It had been a long and involved and emotional discussion in the student center that Sunday evening on the topic "The Christian Interpretation of Sex." Everyone heaved a sigh as the conversation drew to an end and the moderator asked, "Are there any more questions or additional comments to be made?"

To this one thin voice replied from the rear of the room, "Well, I think sex is here to stay."

Yes, sex is here to stay. Indeed, God meant it to be that way. So often we may get the idea, somehow, that sex is intrinsically bad or dirty or that it is somehow involved only with the body — and the body somehow corrupts the rest of one's being.

But Scripture speaks of man as a unity. And God made this unity. Indeed, God made sex. So He must be in favor of it. And this is one of the first clues towards our understanding of this gift of God. God wants you to be the very best male or female that you possibly can be. He created you with your sexuality.

Second, sex has not only to do with the physical — our body — but it is a total union of two people emotionally, spiritually, and from it can come a communion of two personalities which is one of the most beautiful gifts which God has given to man. This total oneness, of course, can be destroyed if one views sex as the only purpose of marriage or for that matter as the primary relationship between a young man and a young woman in dating or courtship. Here, most subtly, if sex is viewed only as a means to an end, two people can become things; human worth and integrity are destroyed, and the real unity of two personalities which could be built up is left in shambles.

The true meaning of sex, then, is understood only in the light of two people as they see their friendship, their courtship, or their marriage under the perspective of God's presence and God's promises. In the self-giving of Christ on the cross, we see the clue towards a proper use of our own sexuality — in denying oneself for the other person and making full use of our sexual powers only within that blessed estate of marriage where God has said He would bless.

Let no one say that God leaves the Christian young man or woman without help in these days of *Sturm und Drang*. God has a promise that really works in this case; it is 1 Corinthians 10:12, 13: "Therefore let anyone who thinks that he stands take heed lest he fall. No temptation has overtaken you that is not common to man. God is faithful, and He will not let you be tempted beyond your strength but with the temptation will also provide the way of escape that you may be able to endure it."

This is a tremendous promise, isn't it? When temptations to impurity come one's way, God has promised that there is a way of escape if we will but look for it. It may mean turning immediately to prayer for God's help in time of testing. It may mean learning how to sublimate and throw ourselves into other activities. It may mean getting the help of another friend who will be able to "hold up your arms" (Exodus 17:12) and give us the Christian guidance and counsel that we need. It may mean simply learning how to run away from the temptation by using those gifts of our two legs.

Most certainly the Scripture is always by our side, and we can turn to it for grace to help in time of need. Indeed the Word of God comes to us again and again with God's promises of help. "Call upon Me in the day of trouble; I will deliver you, and you shall glorify Me." (Psalm 50:15)

A final escape hatch may be one of the most difficult of all to use — simply learning how to say no! But God Himself will give each individual the strength to say no when that individual is immersed in God's holy Word and is using the sacraments penitently and regularly.

So there you are; there are the "ways of escape for you" which God has promised to have available in your hour of temptation.

Sex is here to stay. Indeed, God gave you your sexuality. He will also give you the grace to use it as a blessing. He will enable you to praise Him and serve your future life partner through your sexuality.

The worshiper paused at the front door of the church after the service and said to the pastor, "You know, Pastor, when you start preaching, you are like a surgeon. You cut me open and you take me apart and you show me what a terrible person I am on the inside. And it is a horrible sight to behold. But thank God, by the end of the sermon you've got me all put back together again and all sewed up once more."

In many respects the work of a pastor is like the work of a surgeon. The homiletical formula of goal, malady, and means applies. The task must be clearly seen, the illness diagnosed, and the medicine or surgical skill put to work to solve the illness. And this is what happens in the publication of Law and Gospel to the hearers of a sermon. The Law shows us our sin and our need for a Savior. The Gospel is the good news that God has forgiven our sins in Christ.

Only when we see the radical nature of our sin, our perversity in making ourselves God in so many ways in our daily lives, can we realize what it cost Christ to redeem us from our horrible estate. "Ye killed the Prince of Life." It was God Himself who died, who gave Himself into death for the sins which all of us have committed. Only when we realize the enormity of the price that was paid do we realize how serious the disease has been and how wonderful is the healing power.

A woman once chatted with the pastor at the church door after a service and said, "It was a wonderful sermon, Pastor!" To this the pastor replied, "Well, we'll see."

After the hearing of the Law and the Gospel comes the living of the new Gospel life in relationship with God. James put it this way: "But be doers of the Word and not hearers only." (James 1:22)

"Three Cheers for God"

In his *Plain Christianity* (Macmillan, 1955) J. B. Phillips tells the story of an exciting evening at a youth center in London. There had been dancing, speeches and cheers, and singing "For He's a Jolly Good Fellow." At the end of the evening he suggested that the group have some worship.

One person spoke up bluntly, "You know, we haven't any idea what you really mean by worship!"

"Haven't you?" he responded. "Well, it's three cheers for God!"

So often we may come to church to have our problems solved, to get help for spiritual life, to get our mind off our difficulties on campus, or of course for further more mundane reasons like "it simply being Sunday morning" or "having nothing else better to do."

But many of our problems and anxieties would fade away if we could just get our eyes focused back on the goal of our earthly pilgrimage and on our heavenly Father, who knows all the things that we really need.

What we must do is "lose ourselves" in worship and adoration and praise of this great God of ours. *Adoramus te, Christe!* "We adore Thee, O Christ." This would be our theme song as we extol the wonder and greatness of our loving, beneficent God.

Think of the high points that come in the service, for example, during the Sanctus in the Holy Communion service. The semicircle of communicants standing in the chancel is completed on the other end by a semicircle of angels around the throne of God also chanting in unison: "Holy, holy, holy, Lord God of Sabaoth!"

If we can catch this vision of angels round the throne worshiping and glorifying God — our own task into all eternity — then we are on the road towards the spirit of true worship.

Look at your life this day. This time don't look at the burdens but at the blessings which are yours. Consider such gifts as those that God has given you. Above all, remember that He has given His own blessed Son into death for your sins.

If one has caught the height and depth and breadth and length of God's love for us, how could he help but sing, "Three cheers for God!"

It was a morning convocation during Religious Emphasis Week at Oklahoma State University in Stillwater. The guest speaker had just finished, and the crowd was heading for the doors. A number of students came down to the rostrum. Among them was a Moslem student, who said to the speaker, "I enjoyed your talk very much, but I cannot agree with you as to the exclusiveness of Christianity and your implication that believing in Christ is the only true religion. I believe that the one great theme of all religions is love. Don't you? If a man has love — whether he is a Jew, a Moslem, a Christian, or whatever — isn't that the only important thing?"

It's a good question, and love certainly is the greatest thing that is needed in the affairs of men and nations in this tumultuous age of ours. But a man may "love" and still live a life which ignores God, who is the Author of all love. This is the tragedy of many a life — the "good agnostic," the well-meaning humanist, the altruist in the helping professions, the "good guy" on campus, who may be very selfless in many of the things that he or she does but has never really given God the glory for "the good" which is being done.

Someone has said, "These people are drinking from a stream, the source of which they deny." Again the questions must be raised: Who made you? Where did you come from? What is the origin and source of this power of love and forgiveness which you grant is so needed in the affairs of men and nations?

Christ said: "He who abides in Me, and I in him, he it is that bears much fruit, for apart from Me you can do nothing" (John 15:5). In Hebrews we read: "Without faith it is impossible to please Him" (Hebrews 11:6). And so, much as we respect the "civil righteousness" of men, it is not "good" in God's eyes. Only when God in Christ is acknowledged as the Author and Source of this love is man doing "the good" from an eternal perspective.

For the fountain and wellspring of love was opened up on Calvary that Good Friday when a spear pierced Christ's side, and blood and water flowed forth. It was in Christ's death that the greatest love of all was shown in His giving Himself into the pangs of hell for all of us. From that fountain flows the life-giving forgiveness of sins in the water of Holy Baptism and the body and blood of Holy Communion.

"In this is love, not that we loved God but that He loved us and sent His Son to be the Expiation for our sins." (1 John 4:10)

A Christian student once told me that in his life in a dormitory he had been trying to reach one particular young man who was not a Christian. They had had a number of conversations over a period of months, but one day his friend said to him: "Look, Lloyd, I'm not nearly as concerned as you think I am."

Sometimes Christians may be a little naive in their understanding of "the children of this world." After years of living without God, after years of no contact with Christian people or the means of grace by which God reveals Himself to man, a person may well be able to say in all sincerity, "I don't know what you're talking about," when a Christian begins to discuss Christian truths with him. There may or may not be true atheists, but there certainly are some sincere skeptics, who say, "I just don't know," and some sincere agnostics, who say, "I cannot know absolute truth."

Some of these people indeed may actually have passed the "point of no return." After a repeated hardening of one's heart, God may give one over to a permanent hardness of the heart, as He did in the case of Pharaoh in the Old Testament or in the case of homosexuals referred to in Romans 1:26, 27.

This of course does not mean that the Christian student "gives up" in his witness to all people. Nor should he lose heart in his desire to present the Gospel to all with whom he comes in contact.

Remember the day in Christ's ministry when in His own hometown people refused to believe in Him? The Scripture says He could not do any "mighty work" there but only healed a few sick folk. "And He marveled because of their unbelief."

If the Son of God and Son of Man "marveled" at the unbelief of people who had seen God in the flesh, need we despair when we do not see "results" in our witnessing and proclaiming of the Gospel?

Years ago a lady wrote to Walter A. Maier saying that she had prayed for her husband's conversion for 35 years but now had practically given up hope. What was she to do? she asked. To this Dr. Maier wrote back, "Keep praying for him. Maybe in the 36th year!"

It is not our task to be "effective," "successful," nor always to see the results of our witness on the college campus.

In one sense, it is not up to us to bring men to Christ but to bring Christ to men. It is up to us to be faithful stewards. Man can resist God's call to salvation, but when he does come to faith in Christ, it is God who has converted him.

Let us be faithful in our task as witnesses. God's Word will do its own work.

"Let us run with patience the race that is set before us," the campus pastor intoned from the pulpit. "We glory in tribulations also, knowing that tribulation worketh patience; and patience, experience . . ."

The student squirmed in his pew. "That may be o. k. for you," he thought to himself, "but not for me. Patience! Endurance! I've *had* it this semester!"

But the campus pastor was right, rather, the Scripture was right in saying that the testing of our faith, hard and difficult as it may be to bear, is God's way of perfecting us and equipping us for better service to Him.

A woman, a former surgeon on the staff of the hospital where she now lay as a patient, told me, "This may sound strange to you, Pastor, but I thank God for giving me tuberculosis these last thirty months. In the last ten years, although I was brought up in the church, I had totally forgotten about God in my daily life. Lying on my back these many months has given me plenty of opportunity to re-examine my faith and to get my feet planted again, with God's help, on the road back to God."

Thank God for tuberculosis? It sounds strange, but perhaps the secret is locked up in the rest of the passage to which the student was reacting so negatively: "We glory in tribulations also, knowing that tribulation worketh patience; and patience, experience; and experience, hope; and hope maketh not ashamed; *because the love of God is shed abroad in our hearts by the Holy Ghost, which is given unto us.*" (Romans 5:3-5 KJV)

Ah, there is the key! The love of God will give us the gift of patience. God knows what He is doing, even though we cannot understand it now.

A certain woman was almost totally paralyzed. She lay on an expensive, special hospital bed that tilted back and forth, all day long to enable her to breathe. At night she was taken off the bed and put into a special inhalator, or iron lung. There was no hope for cure for her particular illness; all she could look forward to the rest of her life was this rocking bed by day and the iron lung by night.

The chaplain who ministered to her related that in spite of his many years of work with hospital patients, he had always wondered what he would say if she ever asked him, "Pastor, what is the purpose of my life?"

One day he wandered into the hospital room and overheard her telling another patient sitting in a wheelchair nearby: "Keep your chin up, Sue! Never give in!"

Not only was he struck by the amazing strength and courage of this Christian woman, but he also saw in a flash God's purpose in her life for the years that lay ahead. Here this woman, far worse off than anybody else around her, was giving strength and hope to others who were also ill.

How often don't we complain bitterly about the burdens we bear, as if no one else in the world had the problems that we have! The Scripture, however, reminds us "that the same experience of suffering is required of your brotherhood throughout the world." (1 Peter 5:9)

We also know that God will never give us a burden too great to bear. "As thy days, so shall thy strength be." And Scripture assures us: "And after you have suffered a little while, the God of all grace, who has called you to His eternal glory in Christ, will Himself restore, establish, and strengthen you. To Him be the dominion forever and ever." (1 Peter 5:10, 11)

READ HEBREWS 12

It was a memorable occasion, that festival Reformation service at Grace Church in San Francisco, when Bishop Hanns Lilje of Germany spoke to the assembled throng. He described the horrors of the World War II and the degradations which man has brought upon man at this point in the world's history. He quoted contemporary literature also, showing the fall of man in his bestiality towards his fellowman.

And then he drew himself up after the biting analysis of our decadent age and said in effect: "And in the light of all this, I say that the life of the Christian man in this age should be hallmarked with — joy!"

One would hardly have expected this word "joy" to have come from the lips of a man who had faced almost certain death in a prison cell not many years before.

Here indeed is a stirring testimony from a modern saint, a man almost martyred for the Christian faith, and an example which we must examine seriously and carefully. It may seem contradictory to say, "Joy go with you!" as we see a friend off on a trip or on to some new task or responsibility in a world which knows so little joy and breeds so much hate.

But God has promised us this gift of joy as we do our daily work — a joy and peace that "passes all understanding," a peace and joy that can well up from our hearts and give us the courage to do God's will each day.

Of course, the greatest reason for our joy is in the angel's message that first Christmas night: "Be not afraid; for behold, I bring you good news of a great joy which will come to all the people; for to you is born this day in the city of David a Savior, who is Christ the Lord." (Luke 2:10, 11)

What greater reason for joy could we have than that we have a Savior from our sins! "Joy go with you!"

A young Japanese exchange student, who had been a Christian for only a few years, once told me something I have never forgotten. He stayed in International House, near the campus. In the elevator one day another foreign student, a chance acquaintance of his but not a Christian, remarked to him: "You must have a very wealthy father back home. You are always smiling and seem so very happy."

"He did not know," said the young Christian quietly, "that when I became a Christian I lost my family and my friends; my father cut me off from our family because I had left the religion of my ancestors." He mused a minute, then went on: "I could have told him that the only wealthy father I had was my Father who is in heaven, and the riches of His grace alone have made it possible for me to be a Christian in spite of all the loneliness I have suffered since being cut off from my relatives."

Here indeed was living proof of God's promise that He will be with all those in loneliness and despair, even in heartache such as this, when one has been cut off from his own parents. And this young Japanese Christian lived out God's promise and truth in his life. He was an avid witness for his faith on the campus, a living testimony that God's promises work.

In him the promise of the apostle Paul to the Philippian Christians came true: "My God will supply every need of yours according to His riches in glory in Christ Jesus." (Philippians 4:19)

The glorious truth is that these riches can be the prize and treasure of every one of us. "In Him we have redemption through His blood, the forgiveness of our trespasses, according to the riches of His grace which He lavished upon us" (Ephesians 1:7). Knowing the wealth that our heavenly Father gives us, we can look forward to "the riches of His glorious inheritance in the saints" (Ephesians 1:18), and with this knowledge we have the loving obligation of sharing these riches with others, saying with the apostle Paul: "To me, though I am the very least of all the saints, this grace was given, to preach to the Gentiles the unsearchable riches of Christ." (Ephesians 3:8)

Unlike the rich fool, it is our calling in life not to lay up treasures for ourselves but to be "rich toward God." (Luke 12:21)

One of the oldest criticisms raised against the church is expressed in the comment: "I don't want to have anything to do with the church; I know too many hypocrites who are in it."

The response of a Christian to this comment is the frank admission that there are hypocrites in the church. But beyond the quip, "Come on in, there is always room for one more," it should also be pointed out that there is hardly an organization, a profession, an occupation of any kind which does not have its share of hypocrites.

Two thousand years ago the Bible itself made it clear that "church walls don't make a Christian." Our blessed Lord told the Pharisees in Luke 17:20: "The kingdom of God is not coming with signs to be observed; nor will they say, 'Lo, here it is!' or, 'There!' For behold, the kingdom of God is in the midst of you."

The appeal that we must make to the critic of the church, the one hesitant to enter its portals for systematic examination of the Christian religion, is to look not just at the often bad carbon copies of Christ but at Christ Himself. It must be our challenge to them that they look not just at the organization but at the organism; not just at the denomination but at that living dynamic which is the kingdom of God.

A businessman once spoke to a group of his colleagues and asked them to list their criticisms of Christianity. He listened for an hour as they spelled out their complaints. At the end of that time he said, "You know, all of your criticisms have been against the church and the human beings which make it up. None of you had any complaint to make about Christ. Now let me tell you about Him."

One of my favorite stories has always been the one of the student who every night before going to bed would get up from his study desk, walk over to the window, pull the curtain aside, and say, "Perhaps tonight, Lord?" And every morning the first thing he would get out of bed, go over to the window, brush the curtain aside, look up into the dawn-lit sky, and say, "Perhaps today, Lord?"

This crystallizes for the college student the state of mind which should mark the conduct of his daily life. As one looks at the writings of the New Testament, of Martin Luther, and of other great men of the church, one is struck by the strong note of eschatological tension. So far as they were concerned, Christ was sure to return at any moment with His holy angels to judge the world in righteousness.

The very end of the Book of Revelation says: "He who testifies to these things says, 'Surely I am coming soon.' Amen. Come, Lord Jesus!" (Revelation 22:20)

One of the uncanonical sayings of Christ reads: "In whatsoever employment I may surprise you, therein also will I judge you."

But this business of waiting for and hastening the coming of the day of the Lord does not mean that the Christian student is to be in dread or fear of God's appearance. Truly we are to "fear and love God," but this does not mean we are to be afraid that our salvation is not sure but rather that we are to have all holy awe of our great God and live out our faith in actual deeds of love and service to Him until the day that He lets us see Him face to face.

A grandmother once commented to her grandson, "My boy, see that sampler on the wall? It says, 'Thou Lord, seest me.' Some people will tell you," she added, "that that means God is going to be watching you all the time just to punish you when you do wrong. Don't believe them," she added quietly. "That sampler, 'Thou, Lord, seest me,' really means that God loves you so much He just can't take His eyes off you."

It is in this spirit, with an awareness of a loving God who watches over us at all times, that we await that great day when the Lord Himself shall appear.

The Christian schoolteacher felt he had done a fine job with the seventh and eighth grades as they discussed the topic of temptation. He had made a careful distinction between the words "test" and "tempt," pointing out that often, when the Bible uses the word "tempt," the real meaning behind the Greek word is a testing of one's faith. And the class, he felt, understood that God always gives an individual the strength he needs to bear the burden placed on his shoulders, and the grace to overcome with God's help.

"Are there any questions?" said the teacher as he wrapped up the lesson. A hand slowly rose in the back row, and an eighth-grade boy said, "Well, teacher, I know that God doesn't make us do evil. And I know that He only tests our faith to give us a chance to grow stronger as His children. But, you know, I still think that sometimes He overdoes it."

Some of the greatest minds in history have in effect said the same thing, like the philosopher who said, "If there is a God, He is to be blamed for giving me the reason with which I now reject Him."

But whatever the objection to God or His plan for our lives or the tests and tribulations of faith which He permits to enter the daily run of our affairs, the problem is not that God does not make Himself discoverable or make His help available to us. Rather it is that we do not really believe the mighty promises of God. We don't really make use of the tools of Word and sacrament by which He would apply His power, His strength, and His peace to our lives.

No, we have "a God who is faithful." And He has promised us that if we will but "seek the Lord while He may be found" (Isaiah 55:6), we will find the way of escape that we may be "able to endure it." (1 Corinthians 10:13)

Perhaps at some time a beautiful painting so stirred you that you or one of your friends came out with a sudden, "Oh!" It is this response which so moved the writers of many New Testament books to pause dramatically at certain points and exclaim at the sudden depth of vision they had caught of the great majesty of God as they worked with the divine electricity of His holy Word.

In the ninth chapter of Romans, for example, the apostle Paul is speaking of the great promises of God made to the fathers, and he adds: "And of whom as concerning the flesh Christ came, who is over all, God blessed forever. Amen." (Romans 9:5 KJV)

And at the end of the eleventh chapter he pauses for another ode and soliloquy to the Trinity: "O the depth of the riches both of the wisdom and knowledge of God! How unsearchable [RSV: inscrutable] are His judgments, and His ways past finding out! For who hath known the mind of the Lord? Or who hath been His counselor? Or who hath first given to Him, and it shall be recompensed unto him again? For of Him and through Him and to Him are all things, to whom be glory forever. Amen." (Romans 11:33-36 KJV)

There are times in our lives, especially when the perplexities of our daily tasks confront us with no apparent answer or solution, that we must fall back on this confident note of hope and joy in the all-pervading presence and power of God in our lives.

There comes a time when all we can do is stand in awe of the all-wise, unsearchable God.

"When all Thy mercies, O my God, My rising soul surveys, Transported with the view, I'm lost In wonder, love, and praise."

Just what kind of Christian student are you?

Is your approach to life on campus that of simple adjustment to the pattern of life around you? Have you become so much a part of the routine of things in your dormitory and with your friends that your Christian faith is no longer showing through? Have you so much reflected the moral values of those that you see every day that when people look at you they think, "Well, there must not be very much to Christianity, after all; for that person goes to church, but he (she) is just like the rest of us"?

Or do you live out your Christian life no matter where you are, no matter with whom you are, no matter what the cost? When you are on that big date, when you are chatting between classes, when you're sipping the soda in the student commons, and the opening is there in the haunting, searching questions of those who do not know Christ and the real purpose of life, do you present the Gospel and that One who is the only hope for man's purpose and meaning in life — our Lord Jesus Christ?

In one sense every Christian student will be a loving irritant in his surroundings. He is a "gentle cynic," disparaging the false and self-centered values of a pagan society.

In the days of persecution of Christians in the Colosseum in Rome, the bestial crowds shrieked, "To the lions with the atheists!" The Christians were the "atheists" in those days, for they did not believe in the pagan gods of the Roman emperor.

May we be the right kind of atheists in our own day. May we disturb God's Law but then love others with God's Gospel.

The co-ed was very sincere and well meaning as she explained her intentions to the campus pastor. "I love that fellow so much, I'd just give anything if he'd ask me to marry him. I have prayed to God every night for weeks now that He would move that man in my life to ask me to marry him. If God could let that happen, I would be the best Christian you've ever seen. I would be in the front row in church every Sunday for the rest of my life — my family and my children. This is so right for me! If God will help me out on this thing, I promise God I'll be faithful to Him all the rest of my life."

Does one make "deals" with God? Is the Christian faith a matter of doing nice things for God because He has given us what we want? Even the word "gratitude," which we often use, may well leave some people with the impression that we in effect say to God, "Thank You, God, for all the nice things You've done for me; now look at the nice things I'm going to do for You."

We deserve absolutely none of the gifts God has poured into our lives. God knows far better than we do what we need and what things we should not have for this life on earth. Indeed, God may well bring tribulation and suffering into our lives to show us that we are His children — for a loving father always disciplines his children, and discipline is a hallmark of being well-loved members of a family.

One wonders what this young woman would have done if God did not answer her prayers. Would she then be justified in feeling that God didn't really love her? Was she then somehow absolved from a faithful life of service to Christ? And if the handsome man in her life had married her, just what kind of worship of God would it have been as she sat in that front pew every Sunday morning?

Because of our sin, our rebellion against God, and the fact that we are His children and don't belong to ourselves at all, we deserve nothing from our God except punishment for our sins. But Christ has paid the debt of our sins by His death on the cross; and we are now totally dependent on Him for such good things as He sees fit to give us. Our prayer should not be: "Lord, give me this, and then I'll do that for You." Rather, we will pray: "Thank You, God, for my salvation and all the other wonderful things You have given me without measure. I want to learn cheerfully to accept what You give. Give me that grace."

The attractive girl had been visiting the student chapel for a number of months since coming to the university. In calling on her, as her campus pastor, I encouraged her to become more involved in other activities in the student congregation beyond simply attending the church service.

The girl looked at me with a mock-horrified look on her face and said, "For heaven's sake, don't ask me to get involved any more than I already am in the chapel. I may get to know people better and find that they are just as weak and hypocritical in their faith as I am."

This young lady had an unusual and warped picture of what the church is. She had trotted into the student chapel on Sunday mornings for worship, but, as Luther once put it, she "only held open the sack and received." She never gave back, nor did she get to know other people as objects of her service and love, as people whose burdens she could share. For this is what it means to be a Christian, to "bear one another's burdens and so fulfill the law of Christ."

Further, this girl had a wrong conception of the church in thinking of it as an idealized group of saints who did no wrong. Truly the church is not a haven for saints but a hospital for sinners. Indeed, she would have found weak Christians, even hypocrites in the group. But it was for this very reason that all these people were in the church — oh, to be sure, not the hypocrites; but the weak Christians are there because they want God's help, His love, His forgiveness, the grace He gives in Word and sacraments that they might lead truly Christian lives.

The Lord's Supper, one of God's gifts, is not for the righteous man but for the sinner; and that, of course, means all of us. And "going to church" is not just a matter of "getting that warm feeling" after an inspiring service; nor is it a matter of catching an idealistic vision of people who are "leading the kind of life I wish I could lead." Rather it is an assembly of people who are striving to do the will of God, who confess their sins with true humility, and who with the unearned and undeserved forgiveness of Christ in their hearts go out to face each new week empowered to do better.

The pert, young co-ed shook her cherry-blonde hair and pursed her lips. She did not like what the campus pastor was saying. Back home her father would have said the pastor was "laying down the law to her." So she had skipped church a number of months. That was her own business, and nobody was going to tell her how to run her life.

Of course the co-ed didn't like what the campus pastor had to say. He didn't like to have to say it either, but by his pastoral office he was compelled to bring God's warning and judgment upon one who was despising the means of grace, the Word of God and the sacraments.

And in the proper sense the campus pastor was "laying down the law to her." For only when we see our sin, our neglect of God and His means of grace, only when we see the judgment of God upon our neglect of Him and His love, can the precious Gospel of God's forgiveness have any true meaning at all in our lives.

Only when we see what our sin actually did to Christ, that it cost Him His life on the cross, can we truly appreciate the wonderful news that God has forgiven us, His erring and self-centered and stumbling children.

First the Law and then the Gospel. Whether it's a pastor, a teacher, a parent, or a Christian friend, at times we need to hear them speak the Law to us fearlessly and clearly. And then we will want to hear the Gospel of God's forgiveness told lovingly.

May we be ready with our hearts at all times to hear the Law and Gospel in the right order and in the right spirit.

My Needs? — Or What I Need to Hear?

In *The Churchman and the Social Sciences* Warren H. Schmidt makes the point that man is a need-meeting being and that the church should take this into account as it brings its message to modern man.

One can immediately see the dangers that are implicit in the church simply seeking to adjust its message and its program to the *needs* of men and women. The extreme of this approach in present-day churches has led to a loss of sound theology, to a "psychologizing" of the Gospel, and to turning the church into an agency that simply tells man what he wants to hear or helps him get ahead in business or solve his marital problems.

But Schmidt carefully avoids these traps and still makes helpful use of the insights of the social sciences in telling us about man psychologically and in relationship to other men sociologically.

He points out that God has placed the need for security within us, and to this the Christian Gospel has said, "You are safe. This is God's world, and He loves you."

Man's need of his own self-respect is demonstrated by this, that the individual is told of his importance to God, how God "spared not His own Son but delivered Him up for us all." Here indeed is reason for self-respect, when one knows that he is owned as God's own child.

And the need or drive for self-development and achievement is fulfilled in the Great Commission, which directs and empowers a man to live a creative, service-centered life.

No, the church of God does not simply feed the self-centered needs of pagan man; but it is aware of the nature of man, and the all-encompassing Gospel speaks to man in his every need and condition.

The contemporary novel written by a perceptive literary artist has many values for the Christian. It gives him a better picture of the world he lives in, the world to which he is to communicate the Gospel; it gives him a deeper insight into the nature of other people; and it may even help him better understand himself as he identifies with a central character or a central thesis of the writer.

One Achilles' heel, however, which afflicts many a modern writer's work is that sin, evil, guilt, wrong are often viewed as a corporate condition, and therefore the individual is often not seen as wholly culpable as he should be. By clever dialog and developed polemic, whatever guilt an individual has is seen as "the state of us all." And in such a case one's radical personal sin (and any admission of rebellion against God) is minimized or glossed over.

Joel H. Nederhood has pointed out the result of this treatment in noting that the doctrine of original sin has actually become the great equalizer: "It provides all men with a perfect excuse for their sinfulness." And Edmund Fuller has further described the philosophy in the words: "Neither do I condemn you; go and sin some more."

But Scripture is penetratingly and incisively clear that sin is a personal offense against a just and holy God. And although each individual, like a shoot in a strawberry patch, is connected with other runners and the parent stock, beyond the original, common, sin fluid there is personal, individual culpability for one's transgressions against the holy Law of God.

Thus David said: "Against Thee, Thee only have I sinned and done that which is evil in Thy sight" (Psalm

51:4). And the apostle Paul told the Romans: "So each of us shall give account of himself to God." (Romans 14:12)

Indeed, although we are saved solely by the grace of God, the Scripture abounds with references which demonstrate that man is personally "accountable" before God for his own life.

J. B. Phillips put it aptly in his paraphrase of Romans 6:23: "Sin *pays* its servants: the wage is death. But God *gives* to those who serve Him: His free gift is eternal life through Jesus Christ, our Lord."

It has been said that there was no "new" false doctrine to come into the church after the end of the 4th century. By that time just about every heresy that was possible, in one variety or another, had cropped up in the young church. Ever since then, whatever theological crosscurrents have taken place on the historical stage have been repetitions of occurrences in the early centuries of the church's life, but perhaps only with different labels on variations of the same theme.

No doubt the questions that man has asked about the meaning of existence and his own nature down through history have already been asked years before by philosophers and all those in quest of man's destiny. Indeed, as Ecclesiastes says: "Is there a thing of which it is said, 'See, this is new'? It has been already, in the ages before us." (Ecclesiastes 1:10)

Nevertheless, at this point in history perhaps a certain type of question is being asked by the man of this world with an intensity not typical of earlier times. A century ago a man may have asked, "Why doesn't God *show* His love to me more?" Later the question came: "Is God a *loving* God?" Then came the question: "*Is* there a God?"

But today many people are asking: "Is the question: 'Is there a God?' a relevant question?"

The Christian must deal with the questions which the man of this day is asking. He must "start where he is" and take seriously the concerns and queries which come from the people of our age.

But at the same time the man in search of himself is often asking the wrong questions. Ultimately the Scriptural dictum must be voiced firm and clear: "The fool says in his heart, 'There is no God' " (Psalm 53:1). "Be still, and know that I am God," says the Creator of man. When Job in his suffering cries out to God, "Show me my guilt, O God," God in effect implies that Job is asking the wrong question. For the Almighty Creator of all the universes asks the question: "Where were you when . . . ?" Then follows the whole catalog of creation in the stirring chapters Job 38—42.

Indeed, "it is He that hath made us, and not we ourselves" (Psalm 100:3 KJV). Even as the clay does not point out to the potter the shape it will take, so the Scripture reminds us, "Ye are not your own." "For ye are bought with a price; therefore glorify God in your body and in your spirit, which are God's." (1 Corinthians 6:20 KJV)

Man the creature has often made himself into the creator and therefore is asking the wrong questions. When we in Scripture find the answer as to who we are and where we are going, then we can ask the right questions — and find their answer in the life and person and work of the great God-man, Jesus Christ, for it is in Him that we are to live and move and have our being.

The course catalog for the spring quarter said: "Philosophy of Religion, 3 credit hours." And over 150 students crowded into the modern classroom building to hear the professor's lectures. Many of them felt this was the time they would calmly and "scientifically" examine the claims of religion for their lives.

As the course progressed, it became obvious that this was hardly a study of religions but rather a brief treatment of the "religious" and philosophical views of just a few philosophers in one period of history. A Christian student who asked the professor if the great religions of the world were to be examined, and particularly whether the Christian faith would be discussed, was told by the professor that the course hardly had time for such things.

The broad usage of the word "religious" is understandable, and it is certainly beneficial to study the ideological and ethical views of certain philosophers within the purview of such a course. But in this case many students felt that they had now made a systematic study of "religion," and after taking the course they went back to their regular pattern of studies without further concern for the spiritual or religious implications of college life, certainly with still less interest to examine the positions and teachings of any particular denomination.

The great questions that often go begging on many a college campus are the ontological questions: Who made you? Just where did you come from? Just what is the meaning and purpose of your life?

It is to these great questions that the Christian faith addresses itself as it presents the great God of all history and His mighty acts, culminating in the death and resurrection of Jesus Christ. The student who has never examined the person, life, and work of Jesus Christ during his college career has come out with a blind spot in his education — he is spiritually lopsided.

Even the Christian student needs to reexamine his own faith during these critical days of growth in many new areas of knowledge. The apostle Paul wrote to the Corinthians: "Examine yourselves to see whether you are holding to your faith. Test yourselves. Do you not realize that Jesus Christ is in you? — unless indeed you fail to meet the test!" (2 Corinthians 13:5). And to Timothy he wrote: "Wherefore I put thee in remembrance that thou stir up the gift of God, which is in thee by the putting on of my hands." (2 Timothy 1:6 KJV)

What is it all for? This question should be asked by both the non-Christian and the Christian student during his college days. For the student who wants a complete and balanced education there is no substitute for a thorough and systematic examination of the Scriptures.

The young woman had graduated from college several years before but was still on the fringe of academic life and visited the student chapel occasionally. She sat in the pastor's study now, crying softly, telling of the young man in her life whom she had known and been attracted to, but marriage had not materialized.

The recent romance was now fading, and the young woman, already sensing the failure that lay ahead, was asking for the pastor's guidance in her relationship with the young man. "This may be my last chance for happiness," she sobbed. "What can I do? I want to be happily married like everyone else."

Finding God's will for one's life is not an easy task particularly when the blessings of a Christian marriage which one may desire may not be forthcoming.

Yet, hard as the answer may be to accept, God's "not yet" or even His "no" may be all that some young Christian women are ever going to hear.

We cannot always understand God's ways. But we do know that God is not unaware of our problem, as Paul told the Roman Christians: "The Spirit helps us in our weakness; for we do not know how to pray as we ought, but the Spirit Himself intercedes for us with sighs too deep for words." (Romans 8:26)

Difficult as it may be to understand or accept, marriage may not be in the future for all who desire it. But happiness in a higher and nobler sense can be the gift and blessing of every Christian in the peace that God can place into his heart; for Scripture assures us: "We know that in everything God works for good with those who love Him, who are called according to His purpose." (Romans 8:28)

READ PSALM 139

Coleridge was once asked, "Is Christianity true?"

His cryptic reply was, "Try it!"

For those who want to put the empirical test to the Christian faith, in one sense the Christian faith can stand the test. John 7:17 (KJV) says: "If any man will do His will, he shall know of the doctrine, whether it be of God. . . ." This of course does not mean that one can fit the Christian faith into a rationalistic or empirical box, for the Christian faith is not a dialectic but is suprarational and supranatural.

But the Christian religion is true and gives its own unique "evidence" and "proof." It is true not because it is something that a person has been brought up in, but because *God is true* — for all of us!

Because God the Father is true (and not just because people have wanted and desired the idea of a god), His mighty acts are visible in the affairs of men and nations all down through history. We challenge those outside the church, "Look, He is also active in our lives."

Because Jesus Christ is true, He demonstrated the truth and the power of His love by His sacrificial death for us and His miraculous resurrection from the dead, being God Himself.

Because the Holy Spirit of God is true, He has come and continues to come into our hearts, showing over and over again that the God who created us and continues to support our life, forgives our sins and gives us the power to remain His sons and as remade people lets us start life each day anew.

So to those who question the integrity and authenticity of the Christian religion we say, "Try it! It works." Use the tools by which God reveals Himself to man, and you will have all the "evidence" and all the "proof" that you need.

And then you will receive that divine insight which comes by the work of the Holy Spirit alone: that the Christian religion is true even when it may not seem to work empirically. For the Holy Spirit gives us that miraculous witness in our own hearts that "we are children of God, and if children, then heirs, heirs of God and fellow heirs with Christ." (Romans 8:16)

Several years ago I met a very interesting young man. He was a student at a local Protestant seminary where in the mornings he picked apart Greek vocables; and in the afternoon he picked teeth — other people's teeth. He was a young dentist who had just graduated from the University of California Dental School in San Francisco, a handsome fellow with a charming Chinese wife, and he was preparing himself for God's call to be a dental missionary overseas.

While attending courses at the seminary he hoped particularly to bring the Gospel to foreign students. And if the Lord opened up the way for him and his wife, he said, he would like to go to Singapore or Formosa. Through his job as a dentist he hoped to reach people in a personal way and thus bring his Christian witness to some of the masses of Southeast Asia who still do not know Christ.

So there he was working, preparing himself, open to the will of the Lord, and patiently waiting in line with God's plan for his life for the specific call and direction.

We may be moved to wonder where consecration and dedication such as this is found among our own friends or in our own hearts. We need so profoundly to learn how to open our hearts to God's call. We need to let Him lead the way as we pick our courses, our major on campus, our life partner, everything that we do throughout the months that lie ahead in our lives.

The Lord may be calling you to be a Pete Elliot, a Nate Saint, a Roger Youderian — the missionaries to Ecuador who gave their lives to bring the Gospel to the natives there. Or if not a missionary, giving your life in service for others on foreign soil, then perhaps some other phase of "professional" church work here in our own land. The age-old call is still ringing out, "Come over to Macedonia and help us." It may not only be a call to those who will enter formal training for "professional" church work, but it may be also a call in some specialized field of service which God will yet open up to you.

Meanwhile it is your job as a Christian student to apply yourself assiduously to the task of your daily studies, to work and play — under God — and to learn the mood of the psalmist when he said: "Wait for the Lord; be strong, and let your heart take courage; yea, wait for the Lord!" (Psalm 27:14)

Several years ago the German windjammer *Pamir,* one of the last great sailing vessels of our generation, was adrift in mid-Atlantic in the wake of hurricane Carrie. The ship finally went down, and only six survivors were picked up out of a crew of 86. For some time the ship had drifted aimlessly until finally it went to its last watery grave.

Many students are like that massive German windjammer. It was a stately and powerful vessel, but without guidance and direction it was no more effective for its job than a weather-beaten log also tossed about by the storm.

The student who has no rudder — no chart to guide him through the vicissitudes of life — and who without any defenses is subject to the storms and stresses of life, will ultimately meet the same fate as that great vessel met.

The Scripture says: "We must pay the closer attention to what we have heard, lest we drift away from it." (Hebrews 2:1)

In succeeding verses the powerful witness of the history of the Christian church, and God's mighty acts down through history, is brought forth as evidence. To this we must give our attention again and again, no matter how long we have been members of the Christian church. God's claim on the lives of every one of us and the message of redemption in Christ are spoken of in these words: "It was declared at first by the Lord, and it was attested to us by those who heard Him, while God also bore witness by signs and wonders and various miracles and by gifts of the Holy Spirit distributed according to His own will." (Hebrews 2:3, 4)

Are you simply drifting, tossed about by the winds of life that may assail you? Or is Christ your Pilot and your Guide?

It is an understandable practice — once one reaches Gargantua University — to want to break out on one's own for the first time and really see what other churches and their ministers and their people are like.

But there are also serious pitfalls that can befall college students who simply go from church to church every Sunday. One can easily assume the "observer role" in church attendance: "This is what this church is like, this is what that church is like. This is what I like about this church, this is what I don't like about that pastor."

And if the student goes to his home church on weekends occasionally, there may be the feeling: "Now I am really in the church — this is what I am used to. I know what I like."

But the trouble may be, spiritually speaking, that many of these students only "like what they know." They may fail to realize that Christ's church is found everywhere — wherever His Word is preached in its truth and clarity and the sacraments are administered according to His institution.

The "church" is not just that nice, warm, accepted, and comfortable relationship back at home, but the church is people — the assemblage of Christians wherever they may be found. And it is there, gathered around Word and sacrament, that the individual also has the sacred responsibility to work and grow and give and serve.

May the Scriptural mandate come true in you: "Let us hold fast the confession of our hope without wavering, for He who promised is faithful; and let us consider how to stir up one another to love and good works, not neglecting to meet together, as is the habit of some, but encouraging one another, and all the more as you see the Day drawing near." (Hebrews 10:23-25)

One co-ed was very active in bringing other students to the campus chapel. She always made it a point to speak to her dates about going to church with her.

One week she had a date on a Tuesday night and in the course of the evening invited the young man to come to church with her on the following Sunday. He agreed to come.

On Friday night the young lady was out with a different young man, and in the course of the conversation she also invited him to come to church with her on the following Sunday.

It wasn't until Saturday morning, however, that she realized she had a social problem on her hands. So she phoned the campus pastor and said, "Pastor, you got me into this jam, now you get me out!"

But the campus pastor thought this was a very delightful kind of jam to get into and said, "Well, why don't you bring both of them?"

She did. Both young men appeared in church with her, one sitting on each side. Both eventually became members of the congregation. One of them was killed in naval action during the war.

Another girl in a similar situation got out of it another way. She attended the early service with one student and the late service with the other, neither of the two interested young men knowing about the other.

Then she told the pastor, "If I didn't like the services here so much, it wouldn't be so easy. As it was, I really enjoyed it."

We may smile at the predicaments of these co-eds, but we must commend them for their unashamed witness to their Christian faith.

So often the subject of religion, particularly one's own personal credo, is the last thing that is the subject of conversation on a date.

But the Scripture is very clear that the Christian is always ready to speak of his faith at all times: "Always be prepared to make a defense to anyone who calls you to account for the hope that is in you, yet do it with gentleness and reverence." (1 Peter 3:15)

Indeed, one is not only to defend his faith, but he should not be able to keep silent about "the things that he has seen and heard."

Have you joined the 'secret service'? — Do you "keep quiet about it"? Or are you a gentle and reverent witness to the "faith that is in you"?

The student was completing the devotion he was conducting in the student chapel on Sunday evening before the students went back to the dormitory for one more crack at the books. "And so," he concluded, "we see that love is the motive for our whole Christian life. We love because He first loved us. Beloved, if God so loved us, we ought also to love one another."

"Heresy!" mused the campus pastor to himself. "I understand what the student means, but love is never a motive for action. Love is always action in itself."

Did you ever think of it that way? How can love be a "motive" for anything? Is love a free-floating concept, an abstract principle which one can have in a vacuum without any results and visible evidences of it in our lives?

Scripture tells us that God's very nature is love; but God's love was not just an abstract concept. It showed itself in His great love wherein He actually gave Himself into death for man on the cross. Indeed, the very answer to the age-old question, Why did God create the world in the first place? is found in the response: "Well, God was love. And love always has an object. Therefore God created the world that His love might be shown."

James gives us a vivid illustration of this point when he says: "What does it profit, my brethren, if a man says he has faith but has not works? Can his faith save him? If a brother or sister is ill-clad and in lack of daily food, and one of you says to them, 'Go in peace, be warmed and filled,' without giving them the things needed for the body, what does it profit? So faith by itself, if it has no works, is dead." (James 2:14-17)

So love is more than a motive. Love is always action!

On campus every day other people read "the gospel according to you." God intends you to be a "lively epistle," an open letter to all those around you who are able to read the witness in your heart of your faith in the Son of the living God.

We are reminded of the monk who left the monastery with another, saying, "Brother, let us go down into the village and preach." They wandered down to the village, through the major streets and bypaths, conversing as they went, until they had passed through the village, circled out through the meadows, and were headed back toward the monastery again.

At this point the younger monk asked, "Father, when are we going to begin to preach?" To this the older monk replied, "My son, we have been preaching. We were preaching while we were walking. Our conversation has been noted, our appearance has been observed, the way in which we discussed things with each other was taken note of — and so we have delivered a morning sermon. Ah, my son, it is of no use to walk anywhere to preach unless we preach while we walk."

What kind of "message" do you bring to those around you by your life and by your actions? May you say with Paul: "I have been crucified with Christ; it is no longer I who live but Christ who lives in me; and the life I now live in the flesh I live by faith in the Son of God, who loved me and gave Himself for me." (Galatians 2:20)

In his *Christian Faith and Natural Science* Karl Heim describes the vastness of the universes. One really realizes in plowing through this heavy tome that we no longer have a singular universe but rather a countless series of universes. They are so endless and so numerous that they baffle any human comprehension.

The Christian student sees behind all of this even more evidence of the greatness and majesty and transcendence of God. "He is before all things, and in Him all things hold together." (Colossians 1:17)

The more a Christian student delves into the physical and natural sciences, the more he sees the wonders of God. A search in these fields is a great adventure, for more and more it shows the wisdom and the order of God in His vast created cosmos.

But God is not just "Someone way out there." He was also a human being on this planet in the Person of Jesus Christ, His beloved Son, who said one day: "Zacchaeus, make haste and come down; for I must stay at your house today" (Luke 19:5). He ate and slept and walked and talked with men. — He is "not a high priest who is unable to sympathize with our weaknesses but One who in every respect has been tempted as we are, yet without sinning" (Hebrews 4:15). Perhaps at times we in the church may overemphasize the transcendence of God at the expense of His immanence — His presence here in the world, His presence on the college campus, His presence in our own hearts and lives every day — almost as real as when He walked the paths of Galilee and Judea with His disciples so many years ago.

Almost as real? Oh, to be sure, we cannot see Him face to face as the disciples did, but we have His promise: "If you abide in Me and My words abide in you, ask whatever you will, and it shall be done for you." (John 15:7)

It's an amazing thing, isn't it? The same promises of Christ's presence — of His power, of His comfort, of His peace and pardon that He gave to His disciples before He left this earth — all these promises still hold good for us today.

Christ is alive. His tomb is empty. He is with you and me right now. He is not only the great God of all the universes above and beyond all things, but He is also the God-man who, walking the path of our human nature, took our sins upon Himself and crushed death and hell on the cross. What a great God we have!

Occupation or Vocation?

In his excellent study *The Christian's Calling* Donald R. Heiges makes quite a distinction between "occupation" and "vocation." He notes that occupation is simply the job a person has — but a job with only a horizontal relationship with other people, not a task done to the glory of God.

"Vocation" on the other hand takes into account the totality of a person's life. It is lived within the purpose and the power of God. Vocation gives meaning and significance to all of life, including labor. Even banding bananas in the supermarket eight hours a day can be done to "the glory of God."

Just what is your concept of the lifework that lies ahead of you? Have you chosen your particular course of studies in preparation for a profession that will primarily help you "make your pile"? Have you fully considered the "helping professions," yet not purely out of altruistic motives but rather because thereby you might better be able to serve mankind with your particular gifts and abilities from God?

The day is coming when every one of us will stand face to face with our Creator and the whole record of our life will be laid out before Him. Let us pray that we will not hear the words: "I have not found thy works perfect before God" (Revelation 3:2 KJV), but rather: "And I heard a voice from heaven saying unto me: Write: Blessed are the dead which die in the Lord from henceforth. Yea, saith the Spirit, that they may rest from their labors; and their works do follow them." (Revelation 14:13 KJV)

What are you going to do with yourself the rest of the day? Will every part of it be done to the glory of God?

And how about your lifework? Will it be an occupation, or will it be vocation, under God?

My God Sees!

In a stage play which depicts the story of the life of Joseph in the Old Testament, the temptress at one point tears off her skirt and throws it over the bust of a pagan god in the corner. At this point she calls to Joseph and bewitchingly says, "Now God will not see."

But to this Joseph firmly replies, "But my God sees!"

Hardly a single college student is free of the problem of maintaining Christian purity throughout his days on campus. How does one conduct his sexuality wisely? Is it a matter of knowing that God "sees" all the time, and therefore in fear of a just and wrathful God we go only as far as God's Ten Commandments permit us to go in our relationship with a person of the opposite sex?

God's judgment certainly does come upon those who break His Law. Scripture says: "Shun immorality. Every other sin which a man commits is outside the body; but the immoral man sins against his own body. Do you not know that your body is a temple of the Holy Spirit within you, which you have from God? You are not your own; you were bought with a price. So glorify God in your body." (1 Corinthians 6:18-20)

There is also a positive injunction in this passage of Scripture. The approach to the problem of sex for the Christian is not only a matter of "Don't do this! Don't do that!" Rather it is a blessed realization that one's body is a gift from God and that the Holy Spirit of God Himself reigns within. It involves the holy awareness of the fact that this body was bought with a price, the price of Christ's own death on the cross. Therefore the Christian, knowing of the great love of Christ for him, doesn't just avoid certain things but rather positively does that in his life which is pleasing to God.

READ 1 CORINTHIANS 6

On the bulletin board of a law school in a university on the West Coast there was the terse, posted message: "We do not want you in the legal profession." This note was at once a clue to the overabundance of law students in proportion to openings in the profession, and also a challenge that those who were going to make the grade would really have to "cut the mustard." It also reflected the mood of a professor's comment at an opening meeting at another law school: "Look at the man on the right of you and the man on the left of you. Only one of the three of you will be here three years from now."

The note on the bulletin board and the remark of the professor are understandable in their context. There are other areas in society where membership is subjected to similar stringent qualifications. But it is not so in Christ's church for those who will fully heed His call and commit their whole lives to the One whom the Father sent in His name.

There have been those, even in the history of the church, who have tried to make it a falsely "exclusive" fellowship. There have been those who sought to limit membership in Christ's church by number or even by race. Indeed, there was a congregation at one time which considered a resolution that "membership should be by invitation only." Happily this resolution, which would have made this church more of a social club for "the upper four hundred," never was passed.

There is no limit, no qualification of age, race, color, or social standing, to Christ's call to membership in His family and His kingdom. Indeed, the Bible abounds in invitations that all men might return to the family of God from which they have strayed. God "desires all men to be saved and to come to the knowledge of the truth" (1 Timothy 2:4).

READ ISAIAH 55   94

Most stirring are the words of Isaiah: "Ho, everyone who thirsts, come to the waters; and he who has no money, come, buy and eat! Come, buy wine and milk without money and without price." (Isaiah 55:1)

Who is missed in this invitation: "Come to Me, all who labor and are heavy laden, and I will give you rest" (Matt. 11:28)? "Come, follow Me" (Matthew 19:21). This is the wooing call of our blessed Lord throughout His entire ministry.

"How shall we escape if we neglect such a great salvation?" (Hebrews 2:3). "Let us then with confidence draw near to the throne of grace that we may receive mercy and find grace to help in time of need." (Hebrews 4:16)

One of the most misleading and insidious phrases of our day is "going to church." The point is that this phrase gives the impression that when one goes to a church building or goes to a worship service on a Sunday morning, one is "going to church."

But the New Testament makes it very clear that the church is always people, not bricks and mortar. You and I — we — are the church. Indeed, the laity are still the church of God even though a parish may not have a pastor for a solid year and has called 13 times! I have seen such a congregation rolling along with all guns blazing, when they realized for the first time that they still had the means of grace and God's blessed promise that He was with them, even though their new pastor had not yet arrived.

The Scripture is pointed in stating that the laity are to be subject, not object, in the work of God's kingdom. We can often use words and phrases, though, which perpetuate the false idea of what it means to be "the church" and what the relationship of the laity to the pastor should be. For example, in a church bulletin one might read that the lay people are to be "assistants to the pastor." This is certainly not in keeping with the New Testament, which makes it clear that the pastor is rather to be "assistant" to the people, that he is feeding and leading these people that they might show forth the fruits of righteousness which come from a Christlike life. To this end the pastor proclaims God's holy Word and feeds his people with the sacraments that they might be what they are and have been proclaimed to be under God by Christ's death on the cross.

Richard R. Caemmerer, in his work *Feeding and Leading,* has said that the picture of the pastor in relationship to his people is not that of an engineer who throws the switch on the toy train — and we can see all the people running around the parish at the pastor's direction. Rather it is the analogy of a gardener who is clipping, snipping, cutting, and pruning the lively, growing plant which is the church of God. He nurtures this soil with the sweet milk of the Word of God and the precious healing power of Christ's body and blood. There are as many "ministries" in a parish as there are people in that congregation.

So you are the church.

The man walked up to the airline ticket window at John F. Kennedy Airport in New York City. "Do you have any airplanes going to Europe?" he said. "Oh, yes," said the clerk, "we have a number of flights every day."

"Do they all get through?" the man asked. "Occasionally one makes it," came the reply.

The story, of course, is spurious, but it makes a point. Marriage in our frenetic age is difficult enough already, without adding additional hazards to the venture. When two people of different faiths marry, they have added an additional problem to their relationship which may well be the straw that breaks the camel's back."

But the factor of two people believing differently about the goal and purpose of life — depending on what the religious differences are — is not only "another problem" for the Christian student to consider as he or she contemplates marriage. This is the most important thing for a Christian as he considers a life's partner.

Indeed, Scripture speaks very strongly of the dangers to a person's faith which can come from an intimate association with those who do not accept Christ as their Savior and Lord. There is further the probability that the other person will never change his own religion, particularly if it's the man involved — which man wants to "give in" to a woman? And, third, there are countless case histories of children who are the products of mixed marriages and grow up with confused religious values or no religious values at all as a result of the spiritually asymmetrical relationship.

Because of this triple threat to a God-pleasing marriage, the Christian student seriously considers just when dating with non-Christians has moved into the courtship stage —

when contemplation of marriage is a live possibility. He or she recalls the words of the apostle Paul to the Corinthian Christians:

"Do not be mismated with unbelievers. For what partnership have righteousness and iniquity? Or fellowship has light with darkness? What accord has Christ with Belial? Or what has a believer in common with an unbeliever? What agreement has the temple of God with idols? For we are the temple of the living God; as God said, 'I will live in them and move among them, and I will be their God, and they shall be My people. Therefore come out from them, and be separate from them, says the Lord, and touch nothing unclean; then I will welcome you, and I will be a father to you, and you shall be My sons and daughters, says the Lord Almighty.' " (2 Corinthians 6:14-18)

It has been said that each of us really has four selves. First of all there is your inner self, that self which is known only to you and to God. This is the self which is deep down in your heart; it is your "true" self.

Then there is your self which is your mask to the world: what you see on the faces of other people every day, the way they look to you — and the way you look to them.

Then, third, there is the self that you "ought" to be. And finally, there is the self that you'd like to be.

From the Christian perspective, of course, there may be a big difference between the self that one would like to be and the self that one ought to be. Christ may have very different plans for our personality, and what He would do with our life, than what we would like to do. We may often misunderstand the words of the psalmist: "Take delight in the Lord, and He will give you the desires of your heart" (Psalm 37:4). This doesn't mean that God will give us what we want — or the "self" that we would like — but that rather He will put the right desires into our hearts.

Yes, there's a big gap, a big difference, between the first self of the true nature of our heart and the self that we ought to be under God. Christ is the One who "makes" the difference. He takes over our whole being, and it becomes His temple. Indeed, He has already begun His great work through the Sacrament of Holy Baptism and through the life-giving forgiveness of sins which is ours through faith in Christ.

This is our prayer:

> Finish, then, Thy new creation;
> Pure and spotless let us be.
> Let us see Thy great salvation
> Perfectly restored in Thee . . .

The words of psych lab can be very helpful to Christian students in communicating the meaning and relevance of Christian faith for contemporary man.

"Isolation" is certainly a word that modern man understands. Loneliness is still the biggest problem that plagues all of us, and even in the teeming masses of society we are "lost in the lonely crowd." The root problem, of course, is our isolation from God until we come to know Jesus Christ and fall in love with Him.

"Acceptance." Think of this word not just as the acceptance of a body of dogma as being true but as the realization that we have been declared "accepted" by God the Father, even though we are "unacceptable." Through the work of Christ we can really learn to "accept" other people, no matter how unlovely they may be. For because of Christ's work we ourselves have been made "acceptable" before God.

"Relationship." The Christian faith is not a matter of intellectually assenting to certain truths about God; it is not just a matter of keeping a certain set of Biblical rules. It is a living, breathing, growing, dynamic relationship with God through our Lord and Savior, Jesus Christ.

So there we have it. Man without Christ is in isolation from God; His original sin and his actual sin have separated him from his God. He is a person "having no hope and without God in the world." (Ephesians 2:12)

The doctrines of justification by faith in Christ and conversion by the work of the Holy Spirit are implicit in "acceptance." As Paul told the Roman Christians: "The kingdom of God [means] righteousness and peace and joy in the Holy Spirit; he who thus serves Christ is acceptable to God and approved by men" (Romans 14:17, 18). We are "accepted in the beloved." (Ephesians 1:6 KJV)

In the life of sanctification — that blessed work of the Holy Spirit, of our growing in grace steadily through the use of God's holy Word and His blessed sacraments — is found our "relationship" with God in His own family. Indeed, He is our closest "relative" — He is our heavenly Father (Romans 8:15, 16)

Out of darkness into light into daily growth in the fellowship with all the saints in God's family — thanks be to God for our salvation!

Picture a man standing in three feet of water off shore. He can't swim, but he doesn't worry about it — for at any time he can stand up and walk to shore.

Now picture a man in 30 feet of water off shore. He can't swim either; indeed, he is floundering and will soon go down if he does not receive help.

The analogy holds for the predicament of man — man in any age. Without the help of God he is "at sea." There are those who say there is no help at all, and the sea will soon see just another corpse. But there are also those who say that there is a ship nearby — it is the ship of the church. Indeed, some architectural and liturgical terms in church buildings have naval origin; the "nave," for example, depicts the central portion of the edifice. Entrance into the church of God is through Holy Baptism — and that is why baptistries are sometimes found in the narthex, at the entrance to the church.

But how does one get into the ship? In the Scriptural analogy, you don't climb a rope ladder on the side with your own strength, nor is the life preserver which is thrown out to you a clergyman. Rather, the life-giving circle is the unending, eternal, unchangeable God in Christ Jesus. He is the lifesaver stretched out to you from the ship. And the ship is not a church building — church walls don't make a Christian. Rather it is that holy ark of God's people (for people make the church), of which Jesus Christ is Head.

Man in every age has been flailing his arms in 30 feet of water. But there is a boat nearby, the ark of Christ's holy church; and there is a life preserver, the One who has given His life that all men might be saved.

Imagine the shock if you were to walk into the campus chapel next Sunday morning, and instead of a cross over the altar you would see a hangman's noose dangling from the ceiling. Or imagine your reaction if you were to see a huge electric chair bolted to the wall. The immediate reaction might be: "I wonder which fraternity did this. I don't think it's a very funny prank."

These symbols of death repel us, yet they might bring home to us more vividly the truth that there actually was One who went into the death of a common criminal for us. The cross of Jesus Christ has become so common and is used in so many forms in jewelry and on novelties of so many descriptions that we sometimes forget its true meaning. "Cursed be everyone who hangs on a tree" (Galatians 3:13). Death on a cross was one of the most despicable forms of execution known in the Oriental world. The cross was not accepted as a symbol of the Christian faith for several centuries.

We do well, therefore, to use the cross of Christ in symbolic form very discreetly. We need to remember what really happened on that tree some 20 centuries ago.

A small sign near a display in a religious book store bore the words: "This beautiful gilded crucifix on easy terms." But the cross of Christ does not come on "easy terms." It cost our blessed Lord His own life. It is a reminder that the Prince of Life was killed by man; and "man" includes you and me. But also by that cross we have life with God and so we can exult:

> In the cross of Christ I glory,
> Towering o'er the wrecks of time.

We all know what a thrill it is to get a letter when we are down in the dumps. Maybe your favorite letter is a letter from home, particularly if it contains a substantial check.

One little letter can communicate a whole world of meaning and emotion to another person. One's entire personality can be wrapped up in a letter and bring the reader cheer and joy or sadness and despair.

God cares a great deal about us and has sent us a number of "letters" — the Bible calls them epistles, words of guidance and counsel written by apostles and evangelists to the early church's small Christian congregations. In one sense the entire Scripture is God's "open letter" to all of us. Herein he tells us of His love, His concern, and herein is the Christ cradled who is God's eternal Christmas present to the whole world.

We can write a letter back to God too, for the apostle Paul told the Corinthian Christians:

"You yourselves are our letter of recommendation, written on your hearts, to be known and read by all men; and you show that you are a letter from Christ delivered by us, written not with ink but with the Spirit of the living God, not on tablets of stone but on tablets of human hearts." (2 Corinthians 3:2, 3)

Let's make sure that we are lively epistles as we live out the Christ life, for this is an open letter on campus which is going to be read by everybody. Pray God that everybody reads this letter and sees in our lives the same Christ found in the letters of the Scripture, the Christ who is the Savior of the world.

Several co-eds from different schools were seated together on a train, chattering away as they headed for a Christmas vacation. They were comparing the various rules that their schools had set up in their dormitories, rules that had to be observed or severe penalties would be imposed. The girls compared the schools' differing regulations on how many rules could be broken before a person was "campused" for some time. They all agreed, of course, that there were entirely too many rules, and in general rebelled against what they thought gave them a "hemmed-in feeling."

Every group in society has "rules" of one form or another. We have found that in living together in society rules are absolutely essential for good order, for fair treatment of one another, and to achieve the goals which we have set for ourselves in concert.

Many students, away from Mother's apron strings for the first time when they go away to college, rebel against all kinds of rules wherever they find them. Indeed, they may rebel against any symbol of authority which reminds them of their parents — if their relationship with their parents for some reason was not a pleasant one.

The Christian religion, in addition, may be viewed as a very narrow-minded religion, with all kinds of rules which tie down the individual and inhibit the development of one's own personality. God does have His "rules," His commandments and His whole Law for man's life. He has made us, and it is only right that He should expect us to live according to His way.

But Christianity is much more than a simple matter of "living by the rules." To be a Christian is not just "to keep the Ten Commandments." Rather it is a matter of walking "by the Spirit" (Galatians 5:16). We who are "in Christ" are no longer "under the Law" but are now abounding in the good works which Christ produces in and through us.

Paul described it this way in speaking to the Galatian Christians as he spoke of the liberty of the Gospel:

"The fruit of the Spirit is love, joy, peace, patience, kindness, goodness, faithfulness, gentleness, self-control; against such there is no law. And those who belong to Christ Jesus have crucified the flesh with its passions and desires. If we live by the Spirit, let us also walk by the Spirit." (Galatians 5:22-25)

Think about it. Is your concept of the Christian faith a matter of "do this" and "don't do that"? Or, positively speaking, is it a matter of being a "little Christ" in all that you do, and being a channel of God's Holy Spirit at work in you producing this great list of "fruits of the Spirit"?

The freshman's mother, who was visiting him at the university, had never seen a major athletic contest, and she watched the football game with great interest as the 83,000-strong crowd yelled: "Go! Go! Go!"

It was a hotly contested fight, but one team far outplayed the other, and with only about 10 minutes to go the visiting team led the home team 30—0. Finally the mother in interest and concern said to her son, "They don't have a chance to win anymore. Why don't they just quit right now?"

The mother's comment hardly needs discussion. It calls to mind the comment of another lady who saw two tennis players wildly thrashing back and forth on the court, playing a good, hard game. She noticed, however, that the tennis ball continually hit the net in the middle of the court. Finally in exasperation she said, "Why don't they take down that fool net?"

The games of life and the conduct of the Christian's life have much in common. The apostle Paul several times in his writing compares the Christian's pilgrimage on the earth to a runner, having trained and equipped himself properly for a race, heading towards the goal and prize at the end of the run. Along the course we know that it will not always be easy. This is the exhilarating thing about an athletic contest — the challenge to do our best and to overcome the obstacles placed in our path.

God also in His wise love "tests" His children that they might flex their spiritual muscles and, coming back to the power supply of God's holy Word and sacraments, grow in their spiritual stature and in their realization of need to depend on their heavenly Father.

READ PSALM 94

Indeed, this adventure of the Christian life is hall-marked by testings and trials — by "the ball hitting the net."

The writer to the Hebrews was quoting the Book of Proverbs when he said: "My son, do not regard lightly the discipline of the Lord, nor lose courage when you are punished by Him. For the Lord disciplines him whom He loves, and chastises every son whom He receives." (Hebrews 12:5, 6)

Scripture here uses an analogy which really strikes home, for all of us can understand the necessary discipline of a father who really loves his child. "God is treating you as sons; for what son is there whom his father does not discipline?" (Hebrews 12:7). If we don't receive this discipline, we are illegitimate, not really sons at all.

But our heavenly Father disciplines us for our good that we may share His holiness.

And there is a promise connected with this process: "For the moment all discipline seems painful rather than pleasant; later it yields the peaceful fruit of righteousness to those who have been trained by it. Therefore lift your drooping hands, and strengthen your weak knees, and make straight paths for your feet, so that what is lame may not be put out of joint but rather be healed." (Hebrews 12:11-13)

Christmas vacation was over, and the sophomore walked into her bedroom to start the job of packing to go back to school. She opened her suitcase on the bed, and there they were — the heavy stack of books she had lugged all the way home on the train but hadn't "cracked" once. "Here lies good intention No. 8,563," she mused wistfully to herself.

"Don't do today what you can put off until tomorrow" seems to be the philosophy of many a student. There are just so many things to occupy one's time during the fast-moving collegiate days that often the greatest, most vital tasks remain undone. But all the promises in the world are going to mean nothing unless results come from them.

All promises to God — improving our spiritual life with more regular and meaningful Bible study, prayerfully preparing for and making use of Holy Communion whenever it is offered, really making use of the witness opportunities which God has placed all around us on a college campus — are but hollow phrases if we don't follow through on them. Indeed, Scripture includes a note of warning and serious judgment on those who say one thing to God and do another: "This people honors Me with their lips, but their heart is far from Me." (Matthew 15:8)

How can one change? Try this, and pray over it. As each morning begins, meditate on the Christ who gave His love and life for the student caught in unfulfilled good intentions. Say to yourself, "This day will be spent for Jesus Christ." Check your progress at noon, later in the day, and then before going to sleep say one of two things — really being honest with yourself: "This day was spent for Jesus Christ," or: "Little was done for Jesus Christ."

A foreign student had been in the home of a Christian girl friend over the Christmas vacation. Before leaving for school, the girl's mother asked the international student if she had enjoyed her stay with them. To this the young girl, not a Christian, replied: "Yes, I enjoy my stay very much. But one thing puzzles me. You not have God-shelf in your home? In my country everybody have God-shelf in their house. You worship your God only in church?"

It is an incisive question. Many pagan religions make quite a bit of having a small shrine in the home around which the family gathers for prayers to their pagan gods. So many Christians still have very few things in their homes which are symbolic of the Christian life and of the center of the Christian faith, our Lord and Savior and His cross.

What is there in your study room to let others know that you are a Christian? How might you make use of works of art which would not only declare to others the Christ whom you love and serve but also be rich stimulation for your meditation and a reminder of Him whose you are and whom you serve?

We need to say with the disciples, "Lord, teach us to pray" (Luke 11:1). For we "ought always to pray" (Luke 18:1). We should be "praying always with all prayer and supplication in the Spirit and watching thereunto with all perseverance and supplication for all saints." (Ephesians 6:18 KJV)

We are to "pray without ceasing" (1 Thessalonians 5:17 KJV) and "pray everywhere, lifting up holy hands without wrath and doubting." (1 Timothy 2:8 KJV)

Is there a "God-shelf" where you live? How might you better enhance the "room of your mind"?

"I Vant to Be Alone"

Greta Garbo said it: "I vant to be alone." Many a college student has responded in the same tone to the well-intentioned invitation of Christian students to visit their campus church. Those invited often make it clear they want to have nothing to do with religion, in some cases will even write bitter letters of protest to campus churches that put them on their mailing list. And on the registration card at the beginning of the school year such a student may make the entries: "Race — human; Church preference — Gothic."

Man by nature wants to be left alone by God and by His representatives. Indeed, this is the nature of sin — "wanting to be independent from God." And somehow we can see how utterly "logical" it is from God's point of view: "My child, if you insist on living independent of Me and My will for your life here on the earth, then I must make it an eternal separation from Me in the life that is to come."

A Christian psychiatrist once put it this way: "Man's basic problem is still loneliness. And this stems from man's 'original sin' of self-imposed loneliness and isolation from God back in the Garden of Eden."

Repeatedly Scripture strikes a note of judgment against the man who cuts himself off from God. All through the Old Testament, whenever the Children of Israel strayed away from their God of Israel, repeated warnings and then often dire punishment followed their apostasy. As Hosea puts it: "They . . . separated themselves unto that shame" (Hosea 9:10 KJV). Man is responsible for separating himself from his Creator.

But the truth is that nobody can separate us from God. We can leave the loving care of our heavenly Father —

READ PSALM 130   112 a Christian can fall away from faith. But no one can snatch us out of God's protecting hand — "Who shall separate us from the love of Christ? Shall tribulation or distress or persecution or famine or nakedness or peril or sword? . . . No, in all these things we are more than conquerors through Him who loved us. For I am sure that neither death nor life nor angels nor principalities nor powers nor things present nor things to come nor height nor depth nor anything else in all creation will be able to separate us from the love of God in Christ Jesus, our Lord." (Romans 8:35, 37-39)

Religious Emphasis or Religion in Life Weeks have often been disparagingly called "Nod-to-God weeks." Particularly if the guest speakers had a wishy-washy message, little lasting spiritual effect may be forthcoming in the student body, and the results hoped for will be stillborn. Indeed, some have suggested that to give a halfhearted nod to religion during only one such week is about as innocuous and idiotic as having a Chemistry Emphasis Week or Physics Emphasis Week only once during the year.

But such weeks can still present good opportunities at times for a witness to Christ's Gospel. Take for example the Christian professor at Iowa State who introduced a guest speaker to a hundred freshman girls in his economics class, saying, "I want you to know that I am very happy to introduce this man to you. Many of my colleagues, together with me, feel that the spiritual values of life are very important in the student's academic life. In fact, I spend every Saturday evening preparing for the Bible class which I teach in my local church on Sunday morning. And so I am happy to welcome this guest speaker to our class during this week, to heighten the need for one's spiritual orientation through all of the courses which one takes on campus."

Some professors would violently criticize a statement like this, indeed would question the man's "right" to say it. As Joel H. Nederhood comments in his *The Church's Mission to the Educated American:* "Apparently, the neutrality and the objectivity which governs so much of academic life becomes operative whenever one is biased in favor of Christianity; it does not seem to operate when one is biased against it." (Page 74)

Christian students and Christian professors need to

encourage one another to be bold like the apostles in making clear their Christian convictions, just as the naturalist and the secularist are bold in their so-called "objectivity." This is not to call for illegal indoctrination of Christian truths in college courses but rather to note the legitimacy of stating one's own view when the proper time presents itself. For God's call is a strong one: "You will be a witness for Him to all men of what you have seen and heard" (Acts 22:15). "We are witnesses to these things, and so is the Holy Spirit, whom God has given to those who obey Him." (Acts 5:32)

The "things" of which we are not afraid to speak? "You denied the Holy and Righteous One . . . and killed the Author of life, whom God raised from the dead. To this we are witnesses." (Acts 3:14, 15)

He was a good-looking physics student, and two co-eds, good dormitory pals, thought he was just about the "most." He had been dating both of them off and on; indeed, the dating process had almost moved into the courtship stage.

That night one of the girls prayed to God, "Dear God, I love him so much! Please move him in his heart to see me as his life's partner, so that he will ask me to marry him before I go crazy with all this waiting. I love You, God, and I love him too. Please help me." And the other girl — well, she prayed exactly the same prayer!

Now what in the world was God supposed to do? Here the two of His children, both faithful Christians, and they prayed the same prayer to God over the same young man. God is "on the fence" — how does He decide this one?

Well, of course, the big thing that is missing in the prayer is the phrase without which you don't have a Christian prayer at all: "O, Lord, not my will but Thine be done."

We need to learn the blessing — yes, the blessing — of *un*answered prayer. God knows far better than we do what is best for us. For our prayers can often be wrong prayers and actually should not be answered by our loving God. Our prayers can be wrong when we try to get God on our side in a quarrel or disagreement and try to justify something which is not defensible. Our prayers can be wrong when we try to get God's support for our own carefully laid plans rather than His guidance for what He knows would be best.

God loves us. He knows what He is doing in our lives. He gave His only-begotten Son into death for us. How can He "go wrong"? Your heavenly Father knows what you need. Trust Him!

A student once noted that his political science professor had batted his eyes 70 times in 60 seconds. No doubt this was distracting; we also wonder how much the student got out of what the professor was saying.

Distractions of one kind or another can be a real impediment to a Christian student's prayer and worship life. We remember the story of the Polish juggler who after an airplane crash wanted to make sure he had full coordination. He was relieved when he could read Psalm 23 aloud without a hitch while juggling six oranges at the same time.

Many of us read the Bible that way, or sit in the pew in church, look at the altar or the pastor in the pulpit while we are mentally busy with the term paper for Monday morning, the ironing which is still to be done for the big date, or the processing of any other baggage in our mind which may pop up into our consciousness.

Scripture urges: "Therefore we must pay the closer attention to what we have heard lest we drift away from it" (Hebrews 2:1). Scripture urges us to "attend to the voice" of God, to "attend to His Words," to "give attendance to reading," and to give attendance at God's altar.

Then when we pray: "O Lord, let Thy ear be attentive to the prayer of Thy servant and to the prayer of Thy servants who delight to fear Thy name; and give success to Thy servant today, and grant him mercy in the sight of this man" (Nehemiah 1:11) — when we ask for God's attention to our prayers, the joyous fact is that He has promised to hear us. "If My people who are called by My name humble themselves and pray and seek My face and turn from their wicked ways, then I will hear from heaven and will forgive their sin and heal their land." (2 Chronicles 7:14)

Students in the school of education become quite familiar with "the laws of learning."

One way of stating them is:

The law of readiness — the learner must be motivated to learn by taking into account physical considerations, the interests of the individual, his emotional needs, and using the principle of "proceeding from the known to the unknown."

The law of satisfaction or effect — the pupil must see a satisfying purpose for the material in his own life.

The law of exercise — hardly a spectator, the pupil must put into practice what has been learned.

The law of belonging or association — the material must be seen in relationship to a total body of subject matter.

One can quickly see the relevance of these "laws of learning" to one's practicing of the Christian faith. Man certainly is "ready" for the message of God's Law and then that of the forgiveness of sins in the Gospel; if a man is not deceiving himself, he is aware of his sin and his radical dislocation from God, and his need for "being made right with God" ("justification by faith").

The law of satisfaction or effect is applicable in the joy that the Christian has in his new relationship in Christ. He sees God at work in his own life and, together with the many expressions of confidence and exhilaration found throughout the psalms, says with the psalmist: "Our heart is glad in Him because we trust in His holy name." (Psalm 33:21)

The law of exercise immediately calls to mind the words of the apostle Paul: "Herein do I exercise myself, to have always a conscience void of offense toward God and toward men" (Acts 24:16 KJV). The Christian puts into practice what he has learned; it's not only "head knowledge" but the service of our whole being lived out in daily life.

The law of belonging or association? Whatever aspect of our blessed Lord's life and work we might consider, we see it all culminating in His greatest miracle of all, His resurrection from the grave. Every aspect of Christian doctrine focuses in the death and resurrection of Jesus Christ — the central doctrine of being justified — "being made right in God's eyes" — solely through faith in the meritorious work of our Savior. So the Christian rejoices in the promise: "If you confess with your lips that Jesus is Lord and believe in your heart that God raised Him from the dead, you will be saved." (Romans 10:9)

The president of the Sunday evening student fellowship was thanking the local ladies aid for the fine meal they had prepared for the students. "It was really wonderful to get a good home-cooked meal for a change," he said, "not like the spaghetti we usually get here every Sunday night." And then a look of dismay came over his face as he remembered that the ladies' aid also had fixed spaghetti for the students.

For some strange reason the word "fellowship" has come to be associated with eating a lot of food. Read the word "fellowship" in a church bulletin, and a vision of an endlessly long table laden with hot dishes, salads, and desserts comes to mind. Further, the comment might be made in a church, "We've got to have more fellowship around here!" And somebody starts planning dinners, or at least gatherings at which people are supposed to get acquainted and feel "real good" together.

The New Testament concept of fellowship is radically, totally different. Far from being a stomach-serving operation, fellowship is not even a "good spirit" that you "work for." Rather, in the Scriptural sense of the term, fellowship is something Christians already have. It is that deep spiritual kinship which all Christians have together in Christ, based on that once-for-all act which He accomplished for all men by His death on the cross.

Every person who is a baptized Christian is in this state already. Indeed, he has been in it for many, many years, even as the redemption of the whole world has been an accomplished fact for many years. "To me," said the apostle Paul to the Ephesians, "though I am the very least of all the saints, this grace was given, to preach to the Gentiles the unsearchable riches of Christ and to make all men see what is the plan of the mystery hidden for ages in God, who created all things." (Ephesians 3:8, 9)

This is a "fellowship in the Gospel from the first day until now" (Philippians 1:5 KJV). This is a "fellowship of the Spirit" of God (Philippians 2:1 KJV). Indeed, this is a fellowship of the sons of God who already live as redeemed beings in God's kingdom and don't have to "work for more fellowship around here." For we say with the apostle Paul that our desire is that "I may know Him and the power of His resurrection and the fellowship of His sufferings, being made conformable unto His death, if by any means I might attain unto the resurrection of the dead." (Philippians 3:10, 11 KJV)

And so when we invite someone to the student chapel for "fellowship," it's not just because the dormitory doesn't have a Sunday evening dinner but because we are inviting these people to the eternal fellowship of God in Christ Jesus. "That which we have seen and heard declare we unto you, that ye also may have fellowship with us; and truly our fellowship is with the Father and with His Son Jesus Christ." (1 John 1:3 KJV)

This is the whole purpose of any gathering in the student chapel or student center: "If we walk in the light, as He is in the light, we have fellowship one with another, and the blood of Jesus Christ, His Son, cleanseth us from all sin." (1 John 1:7 KJV)

A pastor was inviting a lady to bring her spouse to the services at the campus chapel. To this the young woman replied, "Oh, my husband is a scientist. And of course he doesn't believe in God."

To this the pastor quietly replied, "That's not science; that's philosophy."

Science per se has nothing to do with the question of whether there is or is not a God. A scientist himself may not believe that there is a God, but that is his own subjective view. The task of science is not to deal with the moral or ethical values of life; that is the task and role of philosophy.

So it does not follow that if one is scientific, he therefore would reject the idea of God. Indeed, it would be much closer to the task of science in one sense to grant the limitations of scientific method and to be constantly open to the discovery of new truths — truths far above and beyond that which we now know with our limited discoveries.

To the one who rejects the idea of God the Christian student says, "Come now, let us be scientific about it. Let us make a thorough and systematic examination of the claims of the Christian religion."

So spoke the Old Testament prophet Isaiah: "Come now, let us reason together, says the Lord: though your sins are like scarlet, they shall be as white as snow; though they are red like crimson, they shall become like wool" (Isaiah 1:18). And the daring promise of Scripture is always fulfilled to those who would truly be open-minded in their investigation of Christ and His doctrine: "If any man will do His will, he shall know of the doctrine, whether it be of God." (John 7:17 KJV)

"Come now, let's be scientific about it!"

The one agnostic was puzzled as he said to his fellow doubter, "Why do you go to hear that fellow preach all the time? You don't believe the stuff that he says, do you?"

"No," said his friend in reply, "but he does."

The preacher they were referring to was unashamed of preaching the Gospel of Jesus Christ. Yet it was not a Gospel of his own making, nor did he have a power from within himself that caused the one doubter to come back again and again to hear what he had to say. We recall the example in the Book of Acts when two of our Lord's disciples were fulfilling the missionary calling with which the Lord had entrusted them, and the Scripture says: "Now when they saw the boldness of Peter and John and perceived that they were uneducated, common men, they wondered; and they recognized that they had been with Jesus" (Acts 4:13). Like worshipers in one ancient Eastern city who had been to a temple the interior of which was filled with burning incense, and who leaving the temple carried the sweet odor with them wherever they went (so that people could tell that they had been to the temple) — so the disciples of Christ bore on them the mark of the great God-man Jesus Christ. It was His powerful message that they declared, and it was from Him that they received the strength for their boldness.

Knowing that God was with them these men could say, as we can today: "Be content with what you have; for He has said, 'I will never fail you nor forsake you.' Hence we can confidently say, 'The Lord is my Helper, I will not be afraid; what can man do to me?' " (Hebrews 13:5, 6)

Because Christ was God in the flesh, with our heavenly Father's own Word of truth for man, they said of Him, "No man ever spoke like this man!" (John 7:46). And so the world says of us as we speak Christ's Gospel with all boldness, "He really believes that, you know?" And this is true, for the Scripture promises: "He who believes in the Son of God has the testimony in himself. He who does not believe God has made Him a liar because he has not believed in the testimony that God has borne to His Son. And this is the testimony, that God gave us eternal life, and this life is in His Son." (1 John 5:10, 11)

As Christ, therefore, is seen alive and at work in His children, His promise comes true: "And I, when I am lifted up from the earth, will draw all men to myself." (John 12:32)

Thank You, God, for searching me out when I was running the opposite direction away from You and calling me back into the circle of Your family even though I didn't deserve Your forgiveness. Thank You, God, for directing my attention away from myself and to my Savior, my Lord Jesus Christ, who has loved me and given me His own life's blood that I might be His own and live under Him in His kingdom.

Thank You, God, for my parents. I may not know all that they have done to make my education possible or, even beyond the material help they have given me, the concern and the prayers which they constantly have for me even though they may be many miles away.

Thank You, God, for my fellow students. Thank You for those who have been of special help to me in so many little ways during these rigorous days of campus life. Yes, thank You, God, also for those whose personality has been in such contrast to mine; I have learned from them the need to be loving, and I have seen the opportunity to be serving — to those so very different from myself. For You have told me that whenever I serve someone else I am really serving You.

Thank You, God, for all of my teachers. I haven't always appreciated everything they have done either, but they are really Your gift to me, I know, and I want to thank You now for all the inspiration and instruction and insights which they have transmitted to me from the great lore of history and current thought.

Thank You, God, for all the other people on campus who make my life here possible — those who serve the meals, those who keep the buildings clean, all the secretaries and other nonacademic personnel without whom this school would not be able to run.

Thank You, God, for the fellowship of other Christians on this campus. I really need my fellow saints, indeed must confess that I have not sought the fellowship of my brothers and sisters in Christ as often as I ought. Thank You, God, for Your church, for all its sources of power and comfort which are found in Christ, its Head. Thank You, God, for the gift of mind and body such as I have. Please, help me to use the talents that You have given me to the best of my ability and not to be discontent because I have not the talents that some of Your other children have.

Thank You, God, for all the many gifts which You have poured into my life without number, the likes of which I cannot begin to name right now. Truly, You are a great and living God, and I owe You all that I am and have.

Thank You, God!

Perhaps you know a consecrated Christian in whose life you have really seen Christ at work. Indeed, you may have spent hours with this person discussing the teachings of Christianity. But wonderful as this relationship was, it still falls short of that which is a *sine qua non* of the Christian faith: to be a living, acting participant in the worshiping fellowship of a Christian congregation.

Without the fellowship of other Christians, without that fire of the faith which glows when Christians meet together, one becomes like a doubting Thomas, and in the isolation which takes place apart from God's holy church one's own faith gradually atrophies and dies.

You can't be a "blue-domer" and be a Christian at the same time. You can't just worship God out under the blue dome of heaven and ignore the whole Christian church which He has established as not only the power supply for your Christian life, where you receive His Word and the sacraments, but also where you have an opportunity to serve others and renew their faith and life by your witness and by your burden bearing.

All the love and concern and dialog that another Christian may share with you in your life together on campus is not enough. Both of you also need the fellowship of Christ's church and the sacraments which are there administered. The Scripture urges: "Let us hold fast the confession of our hope without wavering, for He who promised is faithful; and let us consider how to stir up one another to love and good works, not neglecting to meet together, as is the habit of some, but encouraging one another, and all the more as you see the Day drawing near." (Hebrews 10:23-25)

READ ACTS 3

A man was once caught on a mountainside in a heavy blizzard. He had been stumbling through the snow for some time and could hardly see where he was going. Deep within him was that strong, increasing desire to simply sink down in the snow and let the sweet sleep of freezing to death overtake him.

Suddenly he stumbled on the body of a man in the snow. Electrified by the thought that this person might be freezing to death, he immediately began to rub the man's arms and legs vigorously. Laboriously he got the man back on his feet and putting his arm under his walked with him, stumbling through the snow, until by chance they found a small hut where they were able to get out of the storm and warm themselves.

Only then did the first man realize that in saving the other man he had actually saved himself and kept his own arms and legs from going numb and meeting the fate which was in store for both of them.

Two college students were out making calls during a fall evening, inviting those who had showed a religious preference on their registration card to come to the campus chapel with them. To their quiet invitation one girl replied, "By the way, do you answer questions?" To this the young couple, a little taken aback at the frank question, replied, "Well, yes, we'll try."

And for 45 minutes this girl pumped the two students about what they believed in, what their church taught, and how they could be so concerned about the Christian faith as to go calling on other students.

On returning to the student center the two told the campus pastor, "Say, have we got a lot to learn about our

Christian faith!" And a new study group was formed as the students examined in more intensive detail how they might make a faithful witness of Christ to their fellow students.

"Those who chop their own wood get warmed up twice." It is in losing ourselves for others that we "save" ourselves. When Christ is at work in a man, His promise comes true: "Whoever loses his life for My sake will find it." (Matthew 16:25)

Is there "love in your life"? Whether you are just dating someone, are deep in a rich and meaningful courtship, or are a married student, just how do you view your relationship with the other person?

Certainly all of us want to be loved, and we need the love and affection of another person. Yet this is only part, a small part of a romantic relationship.

Well, then, let's say that to love the other person must certainly be the highest goal and end of our relationship. To deny ourselves, to give ourselves to and for them, certainly this is the noble goal of two Christians in their courtship or dating relationship and then in that noble estate called holy matrimony.

But there is even more. Since there is always a third partner where a Christian man and woman are concerned, there is still another dimension involved where the two sexes meet. I am saying that the ultimate essence of your relationship with this other person is not only to be loved or to love but rather to catch God's vision of what the other person is to be, and to see your role in helping that other person achieve, in Christ, that high calling.

Did you ever think of the other person in that way? The dimension is not only horizontal, but it also involves the vertical, the other person's relationship with God. Everything that the two of you do together must be seen in this light: How can I help the other person achieve God's purpose in his or her life? How can I keep from forcing this other person into a mold, into a stereotype of someone I want to be a certain way and to treat me in a certain way and to love me in a certain way? And, beyond loving this person simply because I love her or him, how can I catch onto the vision of what God wants to achieve in that other person's life?

This is the real purpose that God has in the relationship of a man and a woman together, both before marriage and in it. Everything is seen within the perspective of God's grace and His purpose, not just between the two people involved. This will also involve a total freeing of the other person — a freeing which is possible only if true love is there. Anne Morrow Lindbergh put it this way: "Him that I love I wish to be free — even from me."

Have you freed your partner — in love? Have you caught God's vision of what the other person can become?

A dignified, elderly lady once attended worship services in a congregation made up essentially of young college students. She was very impressed by seeing all the "handsome young men and beautiful girls singing hymns together." Because of the unique nature of the student congregation the minister tried to explain that there was no real opportunity for her to serve in any of the student organizations.

To this she replied, however, that all she wanted to do was just attend the Sunday worship service. "Just let me come in and go out in my own quiet way," she said.

The request of the woman seemed understandable, of course, but in further counseling with the woman far more was found to lie beneath the surface of her remark. Here was an individual who wanted only to receive and whose concept of being a member of the church did not go much farther.

A West Coast pastor once replied to an individual who wanted to join his congregation, "What kind of member do you want to be? If you want to share not only the honors and the privileges of church membership here but also the responsibilities of time and work and financial support, we will be most happy to have you as a church member. Otherwise, we're sorry, but you can't join our church."

Scripture also requires the person who would be a true, working member of Christ's church to "abound" in Christian service.

The apostle Paul told the Corinthians: "My beloved brethren, be steadfast, immovable, always abounding in the work of the Lord, knowing that in the Lord your labor is not in vain." (1 Corinthians 15:58)

He wrote to the Thessalonian Christians: "Now may our

God and Father Himself and our Lord Jesus direct our way to you; and may the Lord make you increase and abound in love to one another and to all men, as we do to you, so that He may establish your hearts unblamable in holiness before our God and Father at the coming of our Lord Jesus with all His saints" (1 Thessalonians 3:11-13). And he prayed that the Philippian Christians would "abound more and more" and be "filled with the fruits of righteousness which come through Jesus Christ, to the glory and praise of God." (Philippians 1:9-11)

This is what it means to be a member of the church. The question is: What kind of church would my church be if every member were just like me?

"Life must go on — I forget just why." So goes a famous line from a work of Edna St. Vincent Millay.

In the daily routine of campus life many a student may feel much the same way. Dragging to and from class, hardly seeing the end of books to read and papers to write and exams to pass, the individual may lose sight of the goal and purpose of the whole affair.

The beauty of a Christian student's study program is that the why of it all is clearly answered in the life of faith under God, in the kingdom of His Son. He gives meaning and purpose to those who search His Scriptures, use His sacraments, and live in daily penitence and prayer relationship with Him.

God has not promised a life without struggle, without doubts, without unanswered questions and burdens to bear. But He has promised enough strength for each day. He has promised the "way of escape" (1 Corinthians 10:13) that we can find a way out of the squirrel cage we so often create for ourselves. He has promised meaning — through His own death and resurrection — in our daily renewal of our baptismal vow, in which we die and rise again to new life in Him.

Life goes on; and we can know why when we say with the psalmist: "Show me Thy ways, O Lord; teach me Thy paths. Lead me in Thy truth, and teach me; for Thou art the God of my salvation; on Thee do I wait all the day." (Psalm 25:4, 5 KJV)

"Whenever you preach," the professor told his class at the seminary, "a little sign could be hung over your head as you stand in the pulpit: GOD AT WORK. For He is speaking in and through you to God's people sitting out there in the pews."

The same is true of every Christian in the conduct of his everyday life. The campus pastor is not the only one who does the preaching. Every member of the body of Christ is an ambassador, a "minister of the Word of reconciliation." Indeed, by your life you either attract people to Jesus Christ, or you drive them away.

GOD AT WORK — when you chat in the Bear's Lair at the student union with other students who do not know our Lord and Savior.

GOD AT WORK — when you study rigorously to prepare yourself for His service, no matter what the particular profession may be.

GOD AT WORK — on that date with the new light in your life you met in Soc class; when you pray silently before every meal in the campus cafeteria; when you chat into the wee hours with that roommate who has asked, "Why are you a member of the church?"

"He who abides in Me, and I in Him, he it is that bears much fruit," said our blessed Lord, "for apart from Me you can do nothing." (John 15:5)

A longtime member of the church made the statement: "I've visited a lot of churches and met many people in my days. And the one thing I think I've missed hearing the most is to have people say: 'What a wonderful God we have!' "

The wise oldster's comments bear careful consideration. During one's collegiate years God comes in for a lot of criticism and complaint. What kind of God do we have? Or even, where is God — in my life? Why does God let some things happen to me? Why doesn't God help me find answers to the questions I have had so long about Him and the world in which He placed me? When is God going to give me a clear answer as to what I should be and whom I should marry and how I can be sure about these things?

Maybe the questions are all wrong. Maybe the emphasis should not be on my problems, my doubts, my complaints but rather on what God has already done for me and revealed to me in the blessed work of His Son, in the record of His Scriptures, in the sacrament of my baptism, and in the host of blessings He has poured out on my life.

When one pauses to meditate on these things, one is moved to say: "What a wonderful God we have!" And somehow, when our attention is focused on God and all He has done for us, the other questions lose their strength, even become irrelevant. Curiosity, concern, and complaint are quelled by the grand view of the great God who has done so much for me and my salvation. He gave Himself into death for my sin. This should be the focus of my daily life. What a wonderful God we have!

Two humanists were sitting in a Protestant church which had a large corpus of Christ above the altar.

The one mused to the other, as he contemplated Christ on the cross, and said: "Ah, He was a great Teacher!"

"Yes," agreed the other, "too bad He never published!"

There is more behind the comments of these two men than the classic tension on a campus as to whether a prof is a good teacher or a good research man, one apt in the classroom or one who makes his primary contribution in laboratory discoveries or literary productions.

The blessed truth about our great Teacher is that He did "publish." He was not only Rabbi, Teacher, of His disciples and all who heard Him. He also published the Gospel, the Good News that He had come to seek and to save that which was lost. The news release at first went out to small groups of people in a small country. Then, after His resurrection and Pentecost, His reporters carried the message throughout the first-century world.

Later the finger of God wrote the New Testament through the apostles and evangelists. Centuries passed, and a Wittenberg professor published the news again in the language of his people. The news release spread again, throughout the 16th-century world, "as if it had been borne on angels' wings," one historian wrote.

Today, through the mass media around the world, men in every clime, continent, and condition hear the headline story of Him who suffered and died and rose again that we might live with Him forever.

He was a great Teacher. And He also published.

Theocentric vs. Anthropocentric

In *The Church's Mission to the Educated American,* Joel H. Nederhood makes three points in a section on "Preaching to the Educated": (1) It must be stressed that God is the Creator. (2) God is a God of judgment. (3) The Christian faith is relevant to the totality of one's life.

These points are extremely significant and have one theme in common: theocentrism, that is, God-centeredness. This is in opposition to anthropocentrism, which points to man as the center of things.

Particularly in the field of higher education, where attention is focused on the world and the men in it, our concern must always be directed towards the Source, the Author and Finisher of all things — our majestic God. The apostle Paul puts it powerfully in Romans 11:36: "For from Him and through Him and to Him are all things. To Him be glory forever. Amen."

Whatever job one has chosen in life, he should remember that God has made the world in which we live, and He alone gives the ability to work in it. This God will return to judge the world, indeed, has this world under judgment in a special sense right now. "He has showed you, O man, what is good; and what does the Lord require of you but to do justice and to love kindness and to walk humbly with your God?" (Micah 6:8)

Knowing this, there is not a corner of one's life in which God in Christ should not reign as Savior and King. For He is "Lord of all."

In recent years the term "relationship" has come into vogue and has moved from the Psych classroom into common parlance in the mass media and daily conversation.

Christian educators have also coined a special usage of the term, speaking of a "theology of relationships." The point is made that the Christian faith has relevance and result only as it is worked out between people, that the faith is not an intangible thing but that it acts in the daily life situations — the relationships — of human beings. An extreme extension of this view has resulted in the "theology" of some groups which implies that religion emerges from people — from groups — and that where you have people who understand and love and accept one another, there you have religion, and "God" is at work.

The latter extreme view has been criticized by Christian theologians, however, who affirm that true religion does not ultimately come from men, no matter how loving they may be, but from God. Further, God's mediating grace is not dependent on people. People are rather a channel of His love and forgiveness and help to one another.

The faith of a Christian student on campus certainly expresses itself in relationship to other students. For one cannot be a Christian in a vacuum. Christianity is "social" in nature, and one needs other people to love, even as Christ loved us and gave Himself for us.

But the primary emphasis must never be shifted away from God — who He is and what He has done for our salvation. The thrust is on Him from whom all things come — the Creator, not the creatures; God, not groups.

More and more has been heard in recent years about "Christianity and . . ." or "Theology and . . ." some specific area of knowledge or academic discipline.

Christianity and psychiatry, as one interdisciplinary area, has received increasing attention as the stature of the psychiatrist has grown in the popular imagination and as the language of his couch and office have become household words. And since all truth is God's truth, whatever has been validly discovered and applied in the field of psychiatry is welcomed by the Christian church. For it is additional knowledge which God has permitted man to learn about himself and the deep, inner resources of his being. Whatever is true about man is true at once in both the Christian Scriptures and the field of psychiatry.

Take for example the statement of the Christian psychiatrist who said: "Man's basic problem is still loneliness — which stems from his original sin of self-imposed loneliness and isolation from God."

This counselor contended that the basic problem of his clients was loneliness — a sense of personal isolation. At the same time, from the Christian perspective, man's problem has always been the estrangement from God which he brought on himself.

The blessed end to the story, though, is that God did not leave man in the solitary prison cell of his own making. In the Person of His Son He took upon Himself the despair of all men, as we see when Jesus cried to His Father on Calvary: "My God, My God, why hast Thou forsaken Me?" Because He suffered all the pains of loneliness and separation that mortal man will ever know, no person need ever be lonely again.

READ 1 JOHN 2

English Lit majors are familiar with the term "the heresy of paraphrase." In literary criticism, care is taken that concepts are not read into an author's work which are not really there. Nor should other value judgments inhibit considering a piece of work on its own grounds.

The Christian religion also should not be judged unfairly through the "heresy of paraphrase." An individual should not approach Scripture with his own preconceived opinions and prejudices. He should not make up his own self-satisfying religion and then look for a church or group which best fits it — and criticize all other forms of Christianity accordingly. In appraising the Christian faith, one should make sure it is Christianity one is evaluating, not a caricature of it.

In every instance one must be certain it is the true, genuine content of the Christian faith one is dealing with, not some substitute or counterfeit replica of it.

Even members of the Christian church themselves are not a completely adequate yardstick by which to assess the merits or demerits of Christianity as the true religion. For Christians, still being sinners, are only "carbon copies" of their Lord and Master Jesus Christ, and often poor "copies."

It is Christ to whom one must turn in examining the Christian faith if one is not to become guilty of the "heresy of paraphrase." It is in His nature, His person, and His work that one finds the answer as to what Christianity is and what it means to be a Christian. And, praise God, it is also in Him that one finds the power to be a "little Christ," one of the many "other Christs" living in the world before men.

An important task of the teacher training student is to learn the art of formulating objectives. A precise statement of what is to be achieved in the learner is important before the selection of the method to be used in the learning process.

Many an education prof finds that his students state their goals only in terms of understandings, or attitudes, but not in terms of "patterns of action," that is, behavioral outcomes in the actual lives of the pupils. The former are important, but mental goals are limited in scope. More important is that an individual "learn by doing" and put theory into practice in the warp and woof of life.

Many a well-meaning young Christian has fallen into the trap of divorcing faith from life. When the fruits of Christian faith have been lacking, many a concerned parent or pastor has been told: "Oh, I still remember my Catechism," or: "I still believe in the church's doctrines."

But there is a big difference between "head knowledge" and "heart knowledge." There is a world of difference between a mental assent to the truths of Scripture and a living out of the life of love and service and self-denial and witness to Christ among others.

As with the functional objectives of the educator, so the Christian faith must be lived out in one's life on campus.

Christ Himself set us the perfect example in this respect. He was fully God, yet fully man. As a man, He not only thought the right thing and prayed the right words but "did the will of His Father" in heaven.

"Never man spake like this man," said the Scripture. But words weren't enough for Christ. He did the Christian deed and actually lived each day in self-giving until the day He gave life itself on the cross.

At a political party's nominating convention it was estimated that it took only four minutes for the latest rumor about a candidate to make the entire circuit of the thousands of people jamming the convention hall.

Indeed, news, whether good or bad, travels fast. And bad news — well, there's the story of the youthful gossiper who was told to put a feather before every stoop in the village, then later go back and pick them all up again. The task was of course impossible, just as impossible as retrieving ill-chosen words of gossip, slander, spite, tearing down of character, once the words are spoken.

Scripture really has some profound statements to make about loose use of the tongue. If our criminal courts do not make light of libel, slander, breach of promise, or similar suits involving carelessly spoken words, we can imagine the seriousness with which God takes the improper use of His name or the destruction of human personality by invectives of the tongue.

The word of warning is clear: "I tell you, on the day of judgment men will render account for every careless word they utter; for by your words you will be justified, and by your words you will be condemned." (Matthew 12:36)

But the Scripture also gives us a word of encouragement and positive guidance: "Let the Word of Christ dwell in you richly as you teach and admonish one another in all wisdom and as you sing psalms and hymns and spiritual songs with thankfulness in your hearts to God. And whatever you do in word or deed do everything in the name of the Lord Jesus, giving thanks to God the Father through Him." (Col. 3:16, 17)

The two students walked out of Wheeler Hall after the exam was over and paused at the head of the steps to light cigarettes. "God damn —" began one of them as he vented some steam over the not-so-good test he had just written.

His companion's face clouded for a moment, then he said quietly: "You know, Norm, when you say, 'God damn,' like that all the time, you should really fold your hands and bow your head, because it's a prayer!"

One can imagine the "double take" collegian Norm made on hearing such a comment. For who doesn't swear, more or less, on campus? And what in the world has it got to do with prayer?

The second student's comments aren't so strange, though, after all. That many other students do something on campus is not necessarily a criterion for my doing the same thing. And as to the expression's being a prayer — well, it's hardly a God-pleasing prayer. But it is plainly and simply asking God to damn something or someone. This we could hardly desire, nor is it within our province to take such a fearful task of judgment on ourselves.

To state it even more directly, it is "taking God's name in vain." And "the Lord will not hold him guiltless who takes His name in vain." (Deut. 5:11)

We can often slip into the habit of using words lightly without realizing fully what we are saying or whom we are hurting. But our great and loving God has by the death of His Son atoned for this sin as He has for all others. When one repents and seeks His help to master the sins of the tongue, God forgives — and God does help.

The blond, crew-cut figure left the sidewalk and approached a few students standing outside the campus chapel waiting for church services to begin. He wore large, dark glasses, which immediately caused sly comments from a number of his friends. "Ah, out on the town again late last night, eh, Paul?" said one of his buddies.

Paul smiled faintly, then commented: "No. You wouldn't believe this, but I was sitting in my room at International House last night preparing for Bible class this morning. If my eyes look tired, it's because I got to reading the Gospel of John in the RSV, and I just couldn't put it down!"

"He just couldn't put it down." How many of us have had the same experience? How many students give God much of a chance to speak to them through His Scriptures with an open mind and a ready heart?

This is not to imply that Bible reading in itself is a gimmick answer to one's problems, that some ecstatic experience can be expected, or even that Bible reading at first may not present more problems and questions than answers.

But God has promised that His Word doesn't return void, that those who seek Him will find Him, and that the earnest, penitent searching of this Scripture will equip a person to be "complete, equipped for every good work." (2 Timothy 3:16)

As one searches this Scripture, he will find "the Christ there cradled" (as Luther put it), who will speak to him in his situation with His own love and mercy. No wonder that a person "just can't put it down." It affords the very lifestream of God Himself, where "men moved by the Holy Spirit spoke from God." (2 Peter 1:21)

READ PSALM 19   145

The student sitting in the campus pastor's study was explaining the purpose for his visit. ". . . and I have no church background at all myself. So when I learned that my roommate is a member of your church, I wanted to find out more about it. Because, you see, that student really has a faith to live by. I want that faith!"

"A faith to live by." When one examines the phrase, it seems strange that "faith" could have any other meaning or use. But many students, when they are honest, must admit that their "faith" is not related to their life. It may be all "head knowledge" without "heart knowledge." "Faith" may have become a matter of believing the right doctrines or saying the proper prayers or "keeping the rules" of morality and ethics which one grew up with as a child.

But none of these are the Christian faith. For this faith is a living, dynamic life relationship with Christ. In the New Testament, faith involves not only knowledge but also assent and confidence, or trust. This faith pervades the totality of one's existence. It affects everything one does. It is at the root of all of life's relationships. For Christ, the Center of our faith, "is all and in all." (Colossians 3:11)

No wonder the student in the pastor's study was drawn to the life of his Christian roommate. For this one knew the Lord as his intimate Friend and "lived Christ" in all that he did. This, in a nutshell, is what it means to "have" the Christian faith.

"And I, when I am lifted up from the earth," said our Lord, "will draw all men to Myself." (John 12:32)

The guest chapel-speaker concluded his remarks. Then a student rose and spoke haltingly, almost painfully: "But if all that you say is true, sir, why is it that there are so few Christians around who really practice the Christian faith?"

It's quite a question, and a difficult one for any person to answer unless he gives a stock reply like: "Well, it's due to the perverse nature of man."

But look at the question again. Then look at what God has given to man.

Above all, He has given Himself into death for our sin. It is almost above human comprehension, such a gift of love. But God also grants the miraculous gift of faith, by which we can "understand" and practice His gracious presence in our lives.

But more! The charter of new life — my Holy Baptism, daily renewed. The Scriptures — God's own message of life to me and in my language. The blessed Eucharist — His own body and blood, assuring me of the forgiveness of my sins. The church — fellow members of Christ's body to strengthen and sustain me and in whose fellowship I find joyous opportunity to serve Him and others. The life-giving channel of prayer and God's own tender admonition: "Ye have not because ye ask not." (Certainly our problem is not that God does not love us or help us but that we don't really believe the mighty promises of God.)

"Why is it that there are so few Christians that really practice the Christian faith?" It's quite a question. Is there an answer?

O Lord of my salvation, grant that I may use the precious gifts Thou hast given me to be a "little Christ" in all things.

In Arthur Miller's play *Death of a Salesman* Willy Loman is a tragic, poignant, despairing figure. The salesman wants so much to be loved by his family, to be "accepted as he is." He thinks he must "wow" them by being a big success, but he still can't get close to them.

Only a glimmer of hope for Willy is seen in the play, as for example when his son Biff has protested that his father should leave his "phony dream" and admit that neither he nor his son are leaders of men. One can sense the desire of Biff to "break through" to his father. He leaves the scene in tears.

Willy turns to his wife, Linda, and with the crashing realization of his son's real affection for him cries out: "Isn't that — isn't that remarkable? Biff — he likes me!"

A psychiatrist has said that every person needs at least one individual in his life with whom he can completely "be himself." We need "acceptance," "relationship," affection.

Many an individual, especially at a large university, may go begging for such a friend and such a relationship.

What a wonderful comfort it is to have the greatest Friend and Confidant of all — our blessed Lord! When others fail us or when we have no one with whom to share life's pains and joys, He is always near.

The beauty of it is that He likes us. He does not like our sin, nor does He overlook it. For it cost Him His life.

But us He does like, and He loves us with an everlasting love. He has declared us "acceptable" — us, the unacceptable. He loves us, the unlovable.

What a joy, no matter what difficulties the day may bring, to be able to lift up our eyes and say: "He likes me!"

A Christian student was assigned to room with another student who was not a member of the church. As he moved into his new quarters and got himself settled, he noticed that one wall of the room was covered with rather objectionable pictures which had been placed there by his new roommate.

He didn't know quite how to handle the situation, was deeply disturbed by the vulgarity and rudeness of the pictures, yet didn't want to be legalistic in his approach to the problem.

What did he do? The Christian student simply put up an artist's depiction of Christ on the same wall. Without any word being exchanged between the two students, day after day one picture after another came down off the wall until the only picture that was left was the picture of Christ.

Somehow the other pictures just did not fit in with the picture of our blessed Lord.

This is Christ's way in a person's life. There are some things which one just cannot hang onto if Christ is going to be the "chief character" in his life. The Scripture says: "What partnership have righteousness and iniquity? Or what fellowship has light with darkness? What accord has Christ with Belial? Or what has a believer in common with an unbeliever? What agreement has the temple of God with idols? For we are the temple of the living God; as God said, 'I will live in them and move among them, and I will be their God, and they shall be My people.'" (2 Corinthians 6:14-16)

These words have something to say not only with respect to the "furniture" in our lives, the things around us, but also the people with whom we are intimately acquainted. This does not mean that the only friends we are to have are to be Christians; for if we did not know and live and work and play with those outside the church, we could never come to understand and love them and bring Christ's message of forgiveness to them.

But when Scripture says: "Be ye not unequally yoked together with unbelievers" (2 Corinthians 6:14 KJV), and: "Come out from among them, and be ye separate, saith the Lord" (2 Corinthians 6:17 KJV), it is warning us against a total identification of purpose and spirit and belief with "the children of this world." There is a balance then which the Christian student must always find with God's help: to live with and love those who do not own God as Father and Christ as their Savior and yet to be "separate" from them as one who follows Christ's way in everything that He does, not the way of those who know not Christ.

The student who remains faithful to Christ, no matter what the circumstances or relationships may be in his campus life, will find this promise of our Lord fulfilled: "I will welcome you, and I will be a Father to you, and you shall be My sons and daughters, says the Lord Almighty." (2 Corinthians 6:17, 18)

The rest of the students at the retreat were downstairs square-dancing. But this young man had pulled me aside with the tugging plea: "Have you got a minute?" And soon his story was tumbling out.

"I get so churned up inside I don't know which way to go. I was real proud of myself this year when I averaged out with a high *C* in school. Then other kids showed me their *B's,* and my heart fell; and some of them didn't even have to try hard, and they made straight *A*'s.

"And I have to work so hard for what I get, I got real discouraged. I guess my pride was hurt. And this same bunch wanted me to go out with them on Saturday night and live it up; but I just don't care for drinking or carousing. And I get so terribly lonely sitting there all alone in the dorm. I've tried to be a good Christian. But there's no call out for good guys this semester."

This young man had a double-barreled problem. But God in His love has help for these and any other problems that will confront him in his academic career.

First of all, Christ encourages us to be content with such things as we have — also the powers of mind and body which are a unique gift from Him to us. Oh, not that we shouldn't make the most of our abilities; but He does not expect us to be someone else. He does expect us to do our very best, with Christ's help (1 Corinthians 4:2). The results are up to God and to His glory.

Although there is often loneliness in campus life, also because one is leading a life of Christian integrity, Christ has promised that we will not be alone. He has assured us of a peace which the world cannot give; therefore our hearts should not be troubled nor afraid. (John 14:27)

O Lord, I'd better not pray this prayer but just once in a while — when I truly am sorry for having made such poor use of my time and wasted so many precious hours over a weekend when I knew there was so much to be done. What can I say when I have done it again and been such an unfaithful steward of all the gifts You have given me — my mind, opportunity for study at a fine school, the encouragement and support of my teachers and parents and friends, and all the other blessings without number which You have poured down upon me?

I really don't deserve Your forgiveness, Lord, but You have said that You will never cast out anyone who comes to You with a truly penitent heart, that You will forgive me if I honestly confess my sin to You and am sincerely sorry.

I know it isn't just Your business to forgive sins, dear God; for my sins of slothfulness have also cost the death of my dear Savior, Jesus Christ. But while there is yet grace with You, as You have promised, I come humbly beseeching Your forgiveness. Give me grace now to make use of such time as I have left, and by Your Holy Spirit inspire in me the diligence to amend my sinful life. Into Your hands I commit myself, also for a night of refreshing sleep, that I might arise to do Your will and do all things tomorrow and during this next week to Your glory.

In Christ's name I ask it. Without His help I just can't do anything. Amen.

Let me tell you what I believe when I confess the faith of the Christian church in the Apostles' Creed.

I believe that God made me and everything around me. I do not believe that the world was a product of chance or of accident but that an incomprehensible, majestic, and all-wise Creator brought it into being by a divine fiat.

Oh, to be sure, I don't have all the answers as to how it happened who knows how many years ago — or in great detail how God accomplished this miracle of creation; but I do know that it happened.

I also know through the revelation of Scripture that God created man a rational being with a spirit. On these points Scripture is very clear. I know that God has also made me as part of this vast creation of all things in heaven and earth. Since I am His creation, I owe Him my whole life and know I can count on Him for His care. Thus I say, "I believe in God the Father Almighty, Maker of heaven and earth."

In the Second Article of the Creed I echo the wisdom of the Wise Men in worshiping "Jesus Christ, His only Son, our Lord."

I believe that Jesus Christ had no human father but was born of a virgin mother by a miracle of the Holy Spirit.

I believe that Jesus Christ was a full-fledged human being, was tempted even as I am tempted, but, differing from me not in degree but in kind, suffered and died on the cross in the great mystery of God giving Himself for man.

I further believe that Christ's resurrection is not a mere "survival of personality beyond the grave," like Plato or Luther or Abraham Lincoln, but that Christ, doing the impossible, proved His deity and fulfilled His promise of power over the grave for us by rising from the tomb on the third day, later ascending into heaven, whence He shall come to judge the quick and the dead.

Further, I believe in a real hell, not just "hell on earth," although plenty of people make that for themselves too. But I believe, on the authority of the Son of God Himself, that there will be an endless separation from God for those who have rejected Christ as their Savior from sin. And one of the most agonizing things about this existence into eternity will be that such self-loving individuals will be separated forever from the God who created them, loved them, and gave His own life to save them from the destruction they ultimately brought upon themselves.

I believe on the other hand in a real heaven, not a box somewhere up in the sky with gold cobblestones and mansions reminiscent of Victorian architecture but, in a dimension at present not grasped by me, a life which in the most basic terms means being face to face with my Maker in a living and joyous fellowship of worship and service which will never end.

In the Third Article I confess my faith in that Person of the Holy Trinity who has brought me into this living faith in God — the Holy Spirit. I believe in what Christ calls His church, the mystical union of all true believers, be they Methodists, Baptists, Roman Catholics, or Lutherans, wherever they hold the central teaching that Christ the God-man alone redeemed men from sin and that one is saved solely through faith in Him.

I therefore believe with Job: "I know that my Redeemer liveth and that He shall stand at the latter day upon the earth; and though after my skin worms destroy this body, yet in my flesh shall I see God, whom I shall see for myself and mine eyes shall behold, and not another." (Job. 19:25-27 KJV)

This I believe, and this I am compelled to state as a Christian.

Many students still cling to the notion that their appraisal of Christianity can take place in a vacuum, that "it's something I'm going to have to think out for myself."

But God has promised that one cannot know of Him and "the things of the Spirit of God" unless he uses the tools by which He reveals Himself to man. Many a student goes on month after month sincerely pleading for a "discoverable God," yet making no real effort to use the means by which God can speak to him: His written Word, the sacraments, and the fellowship of Christians.

Where do you go from here? Now come the "commencement exercises." If you are not doing so already, begin intensive study of the Scriptures, regular participation in the Lord's Supper, and dialog with Christians who are really living their faith.

The following guidelines form a brief commentary on this process. There are no gimmicks here, no easy solutions. For every person it will be different, for each begins at a different stage of spiritual development.

But the tools are there for you to use. Leave them untouched, and nothing will happen. But let God speak to you, listen to His voice, do His will, and you shall "know the truth," know, too, that it is "of God."

1. *Search the Scriptures.* Use a modern translation, starting with the Gospel of John or Mark. Ask God to give you the victory of Christ to rid you of any sin that prevents you from doing His will.

2. *Relive your Baptism every day.* Praise God for His mighty act in claiming you, an orphan, as His very own and receiving you into His royal family through this "washing of regeneration" in the blessed sacrament of Holy Baptism.

3. *Participate in the celebration of the Lord's Supper frequently.* Here is your clue and channel for an active fellowship with Christ. In the blessed Eucharist yield your whole person to your victorious Redeemer, and He will take you, penetrate you, and assimilate you to Himself.

4. *Practice private confession.* The church of the Reformation retained this practice for the great benefits it gives to the penitent. Specific sins may be confessed, or one may make a general confession in private.

5. *Prayer,* like worship, involves our total relationship with God. For specific prayers, don't forget the hymnal and the psalms. Pray with an open heart, asking that God's will be done.

6. *Live out the Christian life,* not only in association with fellow Christians but also in every other relationship and task on campus.

In this whole process depend not on yourself but on Christ. Look to "Jesus, the Pioneer and Perfecter of our faith, who for the joy that was set before Him endured the cross, despising the shame, and is seated at the right hand of the throne of God." (Hebrews 12:2)

He is inviting you right now to a life of joy and service inside His church.

Won't you please come on in?